D1165119

storied weddings

Inspiration for a Timeless Celebration That Is Perfectly You

Aleah & Nick Valley

Valley & Company Events

Foreword by MARCY BLUM | *Photography by* O'MALLEY PHOTOGRAPHERS

GIBBS SMITH

TO ENRICH AND INSPIRE HUMANKIND

First Edition
22 21 20 19 18   5 4 3 2 1

Text © 2018 Valley & Company Events
Foreword © 2018 Marcy Blum
Photographs © 2018 O'Malley Photographers

All rights reserved. No part of this book may be reproduced by any means
whatsoever without written permission from the publisher, except brief
portions quoted for purpose of review.

Published by
Gibbs Smith
P.O. Box 667
Layton, Utah 84041

1.800.835.4993 orders
www.gibbs-smith.com

Designed by Sheryl Dickert
Film development by Richard Photo Lab
Printed and bound in China

Gibbs Smith books are printed on either recycled, 100% post-consumer waste,
FSC-certified papers or on paper produced from sustainable PEFC-certified
forest/controlled wood source. Learn more at www.pefc.org.

Library of Congress Cataloging-in-Publication Data

Names: Valley, Nick, 1980- author. | Valley, Aleah, 1981- author.
Title: Storied weddings: inspiration for a timeless celebration that is
   perfectly you / Nick & Aleah Valley; photographs by O'Malley
   Photographers
Description: First edition. | Layton, Utah: Gibbs Smith, [2018]
Identifiers: LCCN 2018000515 | ISBN 9781423649410 (jacket less hardcover)
Subjects: LCSH: Weddings—Planning.
Classification: LCC HQ745 .V355 2018 | DDC 392.5—dc23

LC record available at https://lccn.loc.gov/2018000515

For Ava and Bennett,
Back and the moon.

contents

foreword

Whether you are planning a wedding yourself, are a friend or relative of someone planning a wedding, or you are a person in the business of planning weddings, if you are picking up this book, you are in luck!

I met Aleah and Nick Valley many years ago at an event in Manhattan and then again shortly thereafter at a luxury weddings conference. They were still newbies in the business and I was well on my way to being a "Yoda" of the weddings world, having been planning them for more than twenty years and having written *Wedding Planning for Dummies.* It was rare to encounter one company, and in this case a married couple, who planned weddings with military efficiency while designing them with an artist's eye, a true right brain and left brain collaboration. I was very impressed with their talents and passion for weddings, but what truly blew me away was just how incredibly lovely they were. Planning and designing events for a living can take a toll on one's good nature, and not everyone survives the onslaught. The Valleys have not only survived but flourished in this arena and their clients, and now their readers, are lucky that they have.

This very beautiful book is as special as the Valleys themselves. Rather than being a blueprint of specifically how to plan and design a wedding, *Storied Weddings* contains a trove of information that will inspire your own creative process. The Collections chapters in particular, are a visual treasure hunt from which the reader can pull ideas and mix and match them for their own story or simply get an idea of what is possible. *Storied Weddings* is far from being just eye candy; it is meant to be used and referenced often. Throughout you will find solid and down-to-earth planning tips and guidelines gleaned from experts in our industry as well as real couples who have gone through the wedding planning process. The concepts are rooted in contemporary wedding mores, but the common sense approach to designing as well as handling sticky issues is timeless.

Reminiscent of *The Artist's Way, Storied Weddings* will give you the gift of finding inspiration in everyday things and mundane experiences.

Recently, with the writing of this foreword very much on my mind, I was walking down the street in New York, and heard someone yell out my name. It was a bride whose wedding I had planned at least fifteen years ago, walking with her daughter of about twelve. After a bear hug, she introduced me: "Honey, this is the lady that planned Mommy and Daddy's wedding. You know all those photos you love to look at? Well, she was responsible."

It occurred to me then, that the Valleys, like myself, are well aware that we are creating heirloom memories that live on in the fabric of a family for lifetimes. *Storied Weddings* is the embodiment of that awareness.

—Marcy Blum, Marcy Blum & Associates Events

introduction

Valley & Company
History and Welcome

Storied Weddings means a wedding that not only tells the story of the couple it's celebrating, but is a celebration that becomes a fond memory for others, one that transports guests to a moment in time that perfectly captures happiness and joy. A storied wedding is a gathering created with the perfect mix of ingredients that represents the couple.

A wedding should be a hallmark for a couple and part of their lifelong story; moments and memories which will be relived during dinner conversations, tokens which will be framed and admired on mantels and in parents' hallways, and traditions that will hopefully be passed on between friends and future generations. Our hope is that *Storied Weddings* will not only be a useful planning and resource guide, but an inspiring gift that will encourage you to look to your favorite dating memories, your family heritage, fond places you've traveled to, music that means something, tasty food that makes you happy, and other bits and pieces of your story that you will weave into your wedding celebration, your *storied wedding*.

We have had the extreme honor and pleasure of planning, designing, and creating floral and décor for some truly spectacular weddings and parties for our clients and our own families and friends formally since 2003, through our company, Valley & Company Events. While we have watched wedding inspiration and planning methods change extensively over the years (from tattered magazine pages and pictures pinned to bulletin boards to online inspiration and social media—present weddings), the one thing that has remained constant is the human element. The sounds of weddings have remained the same: cheers once a couple says "We do," screams of delight when a bride sees a relative who traveled across the world to join in the wedding festivities, the clinking of glasses during dinner, and children giggling and running around under dining tables when the older guests dance the night away. These moments are timeless and will never change with the trends.

FROM ALEAH:

I grew up with an appreciation for traditions and a love for celebration, instilled in me by my parents and my grandma. Long before Nick and I were engaged, I had a stash of wedding magazines and books that I frequently looked to because they were just so beautiful—the flowers, the dresses, the invitations, and the feelings of happiness! Many of those I still have in our office, dog-eared pages and all. I am so grateful that our determination and love for merriment have brought us to where we are today: creating memories event after event and showing our own children that hard work, family, and celebrations are of the highest importance.

FROM NICK:

As far back as I can remember, gatherings and parties have been some of my fondest memories. Whether it was a large family holiday that went late into the night or bonfires in Birch Bay with all of our friends and their families, these were the moments that began to shape my life as I know it now. These moments were always filled with laughter and stories that, even as a kid, I knew were special. There were times that I would sit under the table at big gatherings, listening and observing all of the fun around me. I feel truly honored that I get to have a hand in some of the most important celebrations in people's lives. I never forget that every event represents for the clients one of the few moments in their lives when all of their families and friends will drop everything and come from all over to celebrate them. I can't tell you how great a feeling it is to sit back and watch a dance floor full of people having the time of their lives or a room full of laughter and conversation, knowing that you have a hand in making that happen. Truthfully, this many years later, I sometimes think that I am still that kid sitting under the table at a gathering, getting to take it all in.

We both had an equal hand in planning our own 2003 wedding, which helped us to put our own marks on the day. That really officially started our husband-and-wife approach. Nick was into the party aspect: the food, the music, and the guest experience. Aleah was all about the designs: the look and feeling of the wedding, and what guests would see and touch. That's very much how we operate our business today. That capability gives us the opportunity to provide a unique and welcome experience for our clients and their guests. Valley & Company Events not only represents us, but the "& Company" in our name represents the incredible company that we've met and connected with along the way and the stellar artists and vendors we have the pleasure of collaborating with on our events. We're so glad we made that decision and gambled on ourselves! All of these events and wonderful people over the years have become part of our own story.

For many years we have dreamed of publishing a wedding and entertaining book that illustrates our own styles, but also one that inspires you, encourages you to learn about your own styles and tastes, and showcases a variety of qualities that can be present in so many different types of weddings. We strongly believe that your wedding should be a complementary reflection of you and peppered with as much or as little formality and tradition or fun as you like. Your wedding should not look like anyone else's—it is your celebration, and influences of you should be felt and seen throughout each chapter of your story and your day.

We are extremely proud of the variety of incredible clients and vendors (or artists, as we like to call them) we have the honor of working with each year, and even prouder to showcase variety in these pages—diversity in the stories shared by our awesome couples, distinctiveness in the designs we created, and a potpourri of tips from fellow experts and industry leaders who have shared their knowledge. This book is a culmination of so many years of hard work and dreaming, and we are thrilled to see our vision come to life and to share all of this with you!

How to Use This Book

In the world of weddings, inspiration is virtually limitless. We have carefully collected thoughts and tips, laid out chapters intuitively so you can follow along and truly use our book as a tool, and produced hundreds of images so you can seek your own inspiration.

There are so many trends that crop up each year. Some linger, some fade. Some become the new benchmark for wedding styles for the next few years. These trends can be wonderful and well done. However, we generally find that classic ideas become the ones that truly mean something to couples, stand the test of time, and ultimately keep coming back.

In this book, we share ideas that we hope will inspire your wedding and other celebrations of yours for years to come. We have included designs for everyone to enjoy: from a luscious garden setting to a formal ballroom wedding, from a modern studio dinner to a romantic tented fête, and a festive winery gathering.

Storied Weddings is laid out in three main parts: Collections, Designs, and Real Weddings, with planning guidelines illustrated throughout. Collections features a compilation of images separated into nine sections that act as a template—You'll find tantalizing wedding desserts and fresh and classic ideas for what to serve your guests, breathtaking bridal and heirloom style ideas, along with wedding dress tips, advice to grooms, and photography suggestions for staging your getting-ready moments before you walk down the aisle. We've included some thoughts and images on clever escort cards and favors, a sweet gaggle of flower girls and ring bearers, some incredible ceremony ideas, and invitation etiquette from some of the very best in the wedding industry.

The Designs chapter is an accumulation of scenarios for weddings or parties, along with call-out tips and dozens of photographs that sing to each style. We have worked on these designs for years, and we bring to life unique, fresh, and imaginative color stories, flowers, and dessert ideas cohesively, with distinctive markers true to each different style.

Real Weddings joyfully celebrates the union of five couples who share their stories and advice as they graciously let us publish their special day and the details of their wedding.

Throughout these pages we offer concepts and thoughts we strongly believe in that we share with our couples and clients. We also include sage advice from some of our favorite industry experts, focusing on their specialties. Take notes! They are the best of the best and their advice is truly priceless. Toward the end of the book is a framework guide of questions for you to talk through as a couple to get a jump on your vision.

Having a hand in planning and designing spectacular weddings and social events for incredible people is an honor, truly. It is a responsibility that we as an industry all appreciate. We inspire each other and celebrate beauty and creativity in each other's work. We enjoy playing a supporting role in chapters of a story that will live on and on, hopefully for generations. In our industry, the bar is continually raised and we find ourselves wanting to push the envelope with creativity, experiences, and designs to give our couples that ultimate experience. *Storied Weddings* is your ticket into the insight and the starting thought process that we embark on with our clients and their wedding planning journey.

So, take our lists and tips and think and dream on them. Have FUN with the wedding planning process! We hope your copy of this book will become well-loved, with tattered pages like those decades-old magazines Aleah has held onto, and will be shared with your friends and family as you excitedly plan your wedding. Or maybe the best way to use this book is to cozy up with a big mug of tea or a glass of champagne and pore over each page, envisioning how you can use the ideas for your own day. Keep a fresh Moleskin notepad and a fancy pen nearby. Treat yourself to a flower arrangement and a beautifully scented candle and set up a relaxing space to just kick back and be inspired. Whatever you do, dive in and enjoy!

Finding Your Voice and Your Own Traditions

Deciding on how to tell your own story can feel overwhelming when you first set out on the planning journey. Searching for wedding inspiration can yield hundreds, if not thousands, of images and links for even one particular style. This process will be more enjoyable and feel easier to navigate as you read this book, and you will be delighted as you get to know yourself and your partner through the process. We want you to feel excited and enchanted at the notion of planning your day, not stressed and discouraged.

AVA

It might be a tall order to immediately know what the layers of your wedding day will be—what your stationery will look like, how your wedding vows will be read, what your tables will look like, how long your veil will be, or how your timeline will be structured. Or you may have already decided on many of these components and need to simply polish them. No matter how fresh or deep you are into your plans, stop to ask if your wedding tells your story. Make sure your voice is balanced with as much wedding tradition as you wish.

So how does a couple begin finding their wedding voice? It starts with conversations about your experiences and your likes and dislikes. Here are some sample discussions.

What did we enjoy at past weddings we have attended?

Did a certain ceremony stand out because of its tradition, candidness, or its modernity?

Was happy hour especially memorable because of the seafood bar that represented the couple's love of the coast? Did I love the sense of whimsy the caricature artist added?

What didn't we enjoy at past weddings or events? Were the lines at the bar too long? Was the ceremony not personal enough? Did dinnertime feel rushed?

Do we enjoy being surrounded by an abundance of our favorite people or are we more homebodies who enjoy intimate dinner parties? (This particular question can help guide the guest count, which is an important first step.)

What feelings do we want guests to experience when they arrive at the ceremony? During the ceremony?

What are the three descriptive words we want our guests to feel when they enter the reception?

How do we want our wedding and events remembered at night's end?

Focus on the positive notes that are memorable to you from past events—but drawing from elements you didn't enjoy can be extremely helpful as well. From there, make a list of these items. Add to them and include notes on details that are important to you both.

Jot down colors, textures, architecture, and objects you love and appreciate. Think about a memorable meal, family holidays, weddings past, and bits and pieces of your own life that can potentially be woven into the fabric of the day. For example, does your grandmother's famed recipe for chocolate chip cookies hold sentiment? Why not serve them during happy hour or at night's end with a carton of milk as guests bid you adieu? Do you fondly remember the lobby of the Parisian hotel where you became engaged for its warmth and old-world charm? Replicate elements of it with lighting, flowers, and lounge furniture to bring that special moment to your day. Does a particular old song represent your first date? Hire live musicians to play it before your ceremony. Do your friends all have a tradition at their wedding of a chant or a song or a special dance together on the dance floor? How do you want to carry on the tradition?

There are countless ways to tell your story, and the beautiful thing is that there truly aren't any rules for what to include or omit. This is your wedding, your story.

By mapping out your likes and dislikes and writing a framework of the scenarios and fun ideas for your day early on, you'll be well on your way to planning and designing a day that is special and has your signature written all over it.

While the décor and visual elements of a wedding are oftentimes the most shared or photographed, the vows are truly the reason why everyone has gathered—to celebrate you in your nuptials. We encourage you to remember this and build a ceremony that speaks to your love story, your beliefs, and your personalities.

Work with your officiant to write a program that might include the story of how you met, your hobbies together, and even an endearing or funny story. Your vows can be by the book, or crafted from scratch and written on your own—a love letter to each other.

One of the most thoughtful wedding ceremonies we recall is one where the best man read aloud *Oh, The Places You'll Go* by Dr. Seuss. It was a more formal event, but the smiles that lit up the guests' faces were just priceless. It set the tone for a gorgeous aquarium wedding with whimsical touches like origami boxes the bride handmade as take-home gifts.

Another memorable ceremony was a formal Indian processional. The groom was surrounded by dozens of his friends and family during the barat. Indian drummers and dancing and chanting revelry surrounded him as he walked toward the beautifully dressed mandap. His bride followed in a moving processional where, in an almost haunting fashion, guests were silent and her brother walked her down the aisle, also surrounded by loved ones. The most enchanting music played and their officiant delicately narrated her movement down the aisle. Even though we were the directors of the day, this ceremony stopped us in our tracks for its beauty, simplicity, and for the reminder of what a wedding truly is all about.

Collaborating with Industry Professionals

Finding the proper team to support your wedding dream is also paramount to the success of telling your story. While there are many wedding planning logistics and design tips we will dive into, making connections with established vendors who share your vision and understand your story is of utmost importance to creating your plans and seeing them to life. Trusted wedding pros are worth their weight in gold and can help steer the course of your plans effortlessly and enjoyably. These pros are the ones who continually raise the creativity bar, as they gain fresh, new ideas and vision with each wedding they plan. When you boil down the ingredients of beautiful weddings, you'll find that they really are steeped with a pinch of this, a dash of that, and a big helping of what is truly important to the couple. Finding your team who shares this sentiment is huge.

Jess Levin Conroy, founder and CEO of Carats & Cake, shares her advice
for vetting and working with top-notch vendors:

Prioritizing what matters most is one of the biggest challenges when it comes to planning a wedding because no matter the budget, you have to make choices. Before you start speaking to prospective wedding vendors, figure out what's important to you as a couple and make sure you are properly communicating this to the vendors you speak with. The more you are able to articulate what you would like to have versus what you need to have, the more your vendors will be able to work with you and match your vision to your budget. Sometimes it all comes down to aligning your vision with your budget and then prioritizing within these confines. Invest in the things that matter and make these decisions first so that you are hiring the right team to execute what's important to you. Also, when evaluating businesses you also want to look at the real live events they have done. While inspiration is great, nothing compares to the experience that comes from working on real weddings.

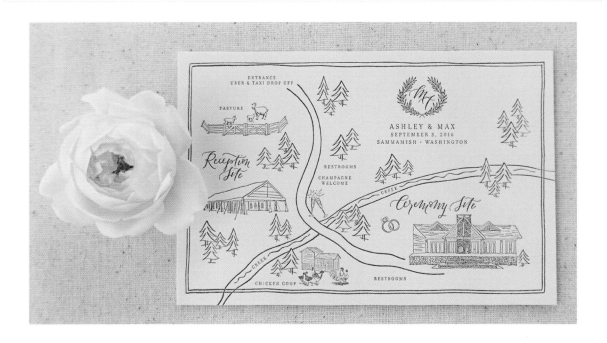

"One of the biggest things is trusting the team you put together, from the florist to the photographer, and giving them the room to use their experience and expertise, essentially giving them the creative freedom to do what they do best."

—Jess Levin Conroy

collections

Weddings and other social events carry a number of layers that include details, traditions, styles, and opportunities for personalization around every turn.

We have captured and presented a variety of ideas and guided advice from defining your personal style to photographing special elements of your style. Enjoy the classic and fresh concepts for wedding desserts, clever favors and escort displays, tips on choosing wedding day music, and a plethora of ideas and imagery to spark your own thoughts and creativity. As with our client designs, we have created styles that we feel are timeless and ones that will translate over different regions, types of venues, and through various aesthetics.

You are welcome to pull our tips and inspiration and use them to formulate your own collections. Think of these Collections as guidelines for what is possible and leverage them into your own ideals.

Invitations & Monograms

Wedding stationery will set the tone for your wedding
festivities and style. The possibilities for stationery are
really limitless—couples can send elaborate invitations
layered in special boxes, invitations inside bottles, an
invitation printed on vellum, or have their menus printed
on fabric or even acrylic. Nothing is off limits when
it comes to finding a personal style for your wedding
stationery. This will also become a tangible piece of your
wedding story that guests may hang onto forever, kept
on their refrigerator or tucked safely away in a box with
photographs or other keepsakes. Stowed securely away
in our office, we have several boxes of stationery suites
and paperie (such as boutonnière and bouquet tags,
programs, and menus) from weddings and events that we
created with our couples and their stationery designers.

DR. AND MRS. WILLIAM BRYANT
INVITE YOU TO JOIN IN THEIR HAPPINESS
AS THEIR DAUGHTER

Abigail Joy

MARRIES

Quenton Joseph Hughes

SATURDAY, THE TWENTIETH OF OCTOBER
TWO THOUSAND TWENTY-FIVE
AT SIX O'CLOCK IN THE EVENING

St. Thomas Cathedral
29 PORT STREET

CELEBRATION AND FORMAL RECEPTION TO
THE BUCKLEY ESTATE

Abigail

KINDLY REPLY BY THE

twentieth of September

Jolien

Martin

First.
CAVIAR WITH CRISPED SALMON
TRUFFLED GOAT'S CHEESE
WITH HALVED FIGS AND HONEY

Then.
SQUASH BLOSSOMS
IN SCENTED RISOTTO

To finish.
POACHED STONE FRUITS
WITH SUGARED GERANIUM CREME
AND SHORTCAKES

Ms. Ceci Johnson
115 WEST THIRTIETH STREET
SUITE 801
NEW YORK, NEW YORK

1 0 0 0 1

Ceci New York's elaborate floral-laden invitation suite is a shining
example of the formality of an invitation and includes layers and
the appropriate components of an invitation suite.

Every year or so we flick back through the stacks and fondly remember why each piece looked and felt a certain way. Whether it was a fanciful multi-layered letterpress and metallic laser-cut suite with all of the trimmings, or an accordion-folded invitation with excerpts from the couple's junior high love notes printed on the back, each piece meant something extra special.

Your invitation suite is a completed collection of paper goods that can include an invitation, an insert with additional information, a map of the locations, a response card, and response details.

The invitation suite itself should represent the style and formality of your wedding so your guests have an understanding of the attire and character of your celebration.

While a wedding "save the date" (sent out six to twelve months before a destination wedding or to simply get on your guests' calendars before details are formalized) can be lighthearted and even funny, it doesn't need to set the tone for your wedding—unless you have a very clear vision early on.

Ceci Johnson, founder and creative director of CECI NEW YORK, explains some of her favorite invitation details:

There are four main "essentials" when it comes to an invitation makeup. The core of an invitation suite includes the invitation itself, the reply card, the reply envelope, and the outer mailer envelope. From there, you can elevate your invitation with unlimited possibilities depending on your unique needs as a couple. The most exciting thing about invitations today is that there are endless ways to enhance the experience, whether it is a laser-cut bellyband that holds all of the pieces together or delighting your guests with a really special, hand-painted envelope liner when they first open your invitation. My best advice is to have an invitation that, first, is functional and clearly communicates all your event information, and, second, tells your unique story through art. It should be an invitation that is a beautiful representation of you as a couple and one that you will treasure forever. When you look back on it in twenty years, all those wonderful feelings of the happiest day of your lives will come rushing back in!

"For a new element, we have been experimenting with holographic foils and printing on acrylic. We have had some really great successes combining a classic watercolor and floral look with really beautiful foiling techniques."

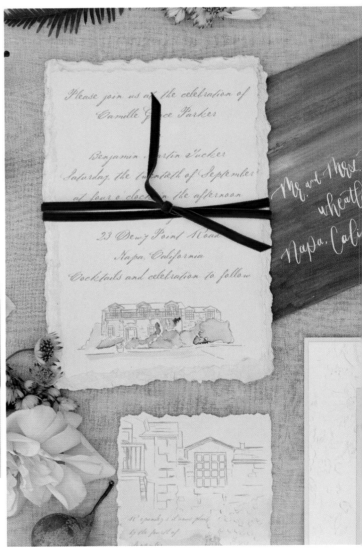

top: A hand-painted whale crest by Libby Tipton tells the story of a couple's love of the ocean. It also becomes a keepsake for them and the emblem for their family.

"If I had to pick a favorite signature touch for an invitation suite, I would choose a hand-painted watercolor and a personal logo that captures the vibe of the couple, especially when that same watercolor appears again on your day. We have used a couple's custom watercolor prints for all kinds of things—from their programs to their dance floor to the pillows or linens at their after-party. Think of it as your personal branding that you can then carry beyond the wedding into your daily life and beautify your world every day."

"Elements of the paper goods can be carried through the ceremony with welcome signage, programs, and vows, to cocktail hour and printed or embroidered napkins, menus, and take-home favors. I've seen menus, logos, and monograms or duograms transferred onto nearly any type of surface—printed onto cocktail trays for the bartenders, carved into an ice sculpture, or made into a floral display."

— Ceci Johnson

The Valley Family
623 Laurel Drive
SEATTLE, WASHINGTON
98105

Kimberly Schlegel Whitman, author and lifestyle expert, shares some of her timeless wedding notions with us:

Monograms are tricky for a wedding because it isn't customary to use a joint monogram (or "duogram") until after the ceremony has taken place. I avoid using a duogram on invitations or programs and save them for reception cards, napkins, and other elements of the reception. My husband and I had our monograms embroidered onto throw pillows that decorated the lounge area of the reception and then used them again later in our home. We also had dinner napkins monogrammed that we continue to use twelve years later.

This invitation suite includes an illustration of the vineyard property for the wedding, winking at the ambiance. The drawing also turned into a memento for our couple—one they can frame and share to mark the day.

"I don't think I've ever seen images of a lace wedding gown or white wedding flowers that I didn't love. Of course, I am a monogram lover, and I think customized details like a monogram or family crest are classic additions that never go out of style. The same is true of incorporating heirlooms, whether it is a grandmother's veil or a family Bible."

— Kimberly Schlegel Whitman

Calligraphy, which dates back to ancient cultures, adds an elegant and personalized touch to invitations and envelopes. Laura Hooper Calligraphy has penned her beautiful script on many of our client invitations, signs, and banners, and the whimsy her calligraphy lends puts a memorable stamp on wedding details.

Think of your invitation suite as the first indicator for your guests as to what your party will look and feel like. Use the paper color and styles to hint at the formality and also to make your guests wonder what's to come. Part of the excitement lies with the element of surprise!

Save a complete set of your invitation suite so your photographer can create a flat lay, which will become a keepsake photo showcasing all of the thoughtful details that went into your invitation.

Vintage postage and whimsical calligraphy is lighthearted and pretty, especially when paired with a patterned envelope liner. A simple initial sticker literally seals the deal!

Mr. & Mrs. Benjamin Langdon
29 Magnolia Lane
Seattle, Washington
9 8 1 1 4

Samuel Peters & Emma Waverly
438 Tangiers Court
San Francisco, California
9 4 1 1 8

Mr. & Mrs. Benjamin Langdon
29 Magnolia Lane
Seattle, Washington
9 8 1 1 4

Venue Styles

One of the first questions that many couples are asked upon engagement is: Where are you getting married? The venue that you choose for your wedding festivities is the biggest underlying factor that sets the tone for your entire wedding experience, from the layout to the implied ambiance, the flow, and logistics for your guests. Selecting that golden venue should be primarily based on several factors, the most important being your styles, guest comfort, and time of year. From there come important details like rules on catering options: Is catering provided in-house or are you allowed to source your own chef? Are there rules for other vendors? Timing restrictions?, etc.

You may want to choose a venue that you can revisit on each anniversary or where you can spend a holiday when you start your own family. It's more than just a place to get married; your wedding venue can become your place.

Seasonality of a wedding is one of the first components to consider when you set out on your planning journey. Do you envision a cozy winter wedding on a snowy mountain? A lively beach wedding in the heat of summer? A springtime wedding that feels fresh and airy? An autumn wedding that features the best of the season? Or something in between? Considering the pros and cons of each season and month will help you to decide on the style of property. Be sure to map out sporting events, graduations, construction going on surrounding the venue and on the way to the property, holidays, ferry schedules, and the like when thinking about venues. Talk to property managers and catering teams about what's fresh in each season for their chefs and what their grounds look like during that time of year. What is their favorite time of year at their property? Getting to know a contact at a venue can help tremendously to learn more about the peak season, the drawbacks and benefits, and the perks of off-season.

Then draw from your vision of style and your own personal tastes to whittle down your list. Choosing a modern spot in the city when you are an outdoorsy couple might not yield the feelings that you envision and likely won't match up to your style.

e

We recommend that couples focus on these questions when they start the venue search:

Does the property offer a turn-key opportunity, where everything is done for you and you just add your small touches? Or would you prefer more of a "blank slate" venue where you can create a totally unique look?

What is the proximity to amenities for guests, such as lodging, transportation, and other activities?

What are the restrictions such as in-house catering and bartending, timing, rules for candles and décor, noise ordinances, and parking parameters?

What is their maximum capacity?

These questions quickly narrow down venues.

This modern lobby and restaurant make for an excellent headquarters for wedding guests—River Terrace Inn, Napa.

top left: Stone buildings bring a romantic charm to this vineyard property in Napa—Whetstone Wine Cellar.

above and left: The grounds at Ramekins in Sonoma, California, set the tone for an unforgettable charming wedding surrounded by vines and terra-cotta.

opposite: A breathtaking island resort steeped in history nestled northwest of Seattle provides endless weekend activities for guests and a postcard setting for a wedding— Roche Harbor Resort.

Identifying your style should be a first step in choosing those venues that match. From wineries to downtown hotel properties, secluded island resorts, tropical destinations, private estates, farms or barns, or a grand ballroom, an urban warehouse, a breezy beachfront, an art museum, or a casual restaurant, there really is a venue for every type of couple and virtually any style of wedding.

Considering the aesthetic of your wedding vision, look to properties that will only enhance your canvas rather than pose extreme challenges in creating the look and feeling that you desire.

Many of our couples choose to marry at a private property or family home (non-venues). These weddings have been one of our specialties from the beginning—creating a layered celebration out of a field or a yard that is a blank canvas. For this style of property, we always first answer these questions—emphasizing the following logistical points:

Is there a level, open area that can accommodate the guest count you are inviting? Is there space for a tent to be staked or weighted? (If staking a tent, the property will need to be flagged for sprinkler systems or underground power—call before you dig!) No matter the weather forecast, a tent can provide shade from the sun, cover from the rain, warmth from the cold, and a definition of space that can be dressed and transformed to become a spectacular backdrop for the festivities.

POWER: *What does the grid look like and will it have the capacity to accommodate lighting, tent heaters, a band or DJ's equipment, catering necessities? We recommend renting separate generators that can run some of these items independently. Surprisingly, coffee urns can set off a breaker over and over again!*

PARKING: *Is there a space that will allow for easy parking and turnaround for guests or a valet service? If not, is there a school or church parking lot nearby that guests can access? Even if there is nearby parking, consider shuttling guests. We generally recommend our clients opt to shuttle their guests to and from select locations to the wedding. Not only does it alleviate possibilities of traffic and directional issues, but it allows guests to feel well*

taken care of. They can simply show up and hop on and off of a shuttle.

POWDER ROOMS: *Is the property on a septic system? Reserving restroom trailers is a viable option that will provide an illuminated, temperature controlled, and water-plumbed restroom. These come in many varieties, including two- or three-stall. These restrooms also help to eliminate lines and you can provide added comfort by stocking them full of amenities like bottled water, mints, and mouth wash. We have found them to be available throughout most of the country. If you can't find a company that specializes in them in your area, look to a construction rental company.*

PARTY: *What are the restrictions that accompany the property: are there noise ordinances, fire bans, close neighbors, and potentials for back-up plans in case of inclement weather?*

CATERING: *Many caterers will opt to pop up a mobile kitchen where they bring in cooling and warming systems or grills and all of their scullery. Making sure there is sufficient space for this by doing a catering walk-through is extremely helpful. Supplying ample power will be important. Walk through the entire property as the guests will experience it so that your caterer knows the exact map and layout of the day.*

While these logistics aren't the most exciting to consider, they are all extremely important and valid and truly can make or break the smooth success of a wedding at this type of property.

Finally, obtaining an insurance policy is a must for any type of wedding, particularly at one's home. This can be done either through your personal insurance carrier (though talk with your agent about whether use of this policy would increase your overall premium), or through a number of online event insurance websites. You can choose your policy limits and the number of days of the policy (for events that have multi-day installations and deliveries, we suggest opting for coverage for all of these days). By answering the questions of what you envision pertaining to your wedding venue and taking note to the five logistical points above, you have hopefully whittled down your venue list and can pencil in a date and location.

Photos of the surrounding nature can help to tell your wedding story and add vibrancy to your finished photos and album. Whether it's rolling hills of grapevines, the silhouettes of boats docked in a marina at sunset, tall cedar trees shadowing a ceremony space, or the city skyline, your photographer will likely snap these images as part of your story—be sure to communicate your desire for these scenic snaps.

right: The glowing marina and surrounding scenery at Roche Harbor at sunset provides such a picturesque backdrop to a wedding.

Ceremony, Flower Girls & Ring Bearers

Wedding ceremonies have dated back centuries and are an important and unforgettable instant where your bond deepens. Your wedding ceremony becomes that moment— the moment in time you and your guests have been waiting for, when you seal your courtship with "we do." Wedding ceremonies can take place in a courthouse surrounded by only witnesses, in large churches with formal masses, be presided over by a relative, a judge, or a pastor, and can include traditional readings, scriptures, poems, or even excerpts from your favorite book. Wedding ceremonies can be as traditional or as nontraditional as you can conjure. A wedding ceremony is perhaps the most personal component of a wedding day and should be designed around your beliefs and your expectations for this special moment.

Of the wild red leaves,
Love, with little hands,
Comes and touches you
With a thousand memories,
And asks you
Beautiful, unanswered questions
~ Carl Sandburg

Margaret & Camden
The Twentieth of June

Some couples opt to have a large group of their wedding party standing by their sides, while others prefer to stand with a sibling or solo. Some brides or grooms walk down the aisle flanked by their parents or grandparents, or by best friends or mentors. Whoever you choose to support you on this journey down the aisle, it is a role of honor.

When plotting your wedding ceremony and surrounding details, don't be shy to put romantic touches on it, or to be as edited as your comfort level will allow. Your wedding ceremony truly sets the tone for your wedding and starting off with your own flair is important. Personally, we opted to read the traditional wedding vows—for us the words that have been uttered aloud at so many ceremonies before us gave us that great sense of tradition in our own ceremony. Every other detail throughout our day was very Nick and Aleah, but the ceremony felt right being classic.

opposite: Flower girls and ring bearers bring an air of play-fulness to a ceremony. Often unexpected, who knows if they'll toss petals and carry rings as rehearsed, or if they'll all skip or dart down the aisle to the laughter of guests!

left: A wedding program is marked with the couple's monogram, signifying the start of their new life together. Passing out programs in baskets or on trays decorated with flowers is not only beautiful, but just a lovely idea. Having them passed out by a special relative or friend who can also greet guests with a smile is even lovelier!

Sarah C. Campbell, founder of Intrigue Design, shares some thoughts about her favorite kind of wedding moments using flowers:

To me, bridesmaids' bouquets are truly timeless. As styles change and trends come and go, the one constant continues to be elegant maids all in a row holding beautiful bunches of blooms. Peonies have a special place in my heart for their sweet scent and timeless look.

As a lover of flowers, I always gravitate toward bouquets, and the bridal bouquet is certainly the crown jewel of wedding traditions. I love the way modern brides and grooms have taken this classic tradition and given it their own twist using creative flowers.

For this wintry wedding ceremony, we created a stately yet whimsical aisle with fluffy flowers and white cherry blossoms seemingly sprouting from the ground.

Ceremony, Flower Girls & Ring Bearers *59*

A paper banner with the words "love as deep as the sea" created a playful vignette at this oceanside wedding—we placed the banner on a wreath and tied it to a white picket fence near the bar. It became its own focal point, perched next to the bar, and an instant photo opp.

"My favorite floral style is 'abundance.' This means I like a lot of everything. If 30 peonies are pretty, 300 peonies are spectacular. This love of abundance has helped define my personal style."

—Sarah C. Campbell

above left: An example of a welcome statement piece, this silver tree arrangement with velvety silver leaves nods to Aleah's Norwegian side (her maiden last name translates to silver tree).

above: An accompanying boutonnière rests nearby which echoes the greenery and silvery leaves in the arrangement.

left: Aleah hand-sewed this ring bearer pillow out of an icy blue cotton fabric and finished it with silk ribbon, which perfectly coordinated with the bridesmaids' flowing gowns and the colors of the day.

Style & Heirlooms

Finding your own comfortable style can help to set the tone of your wedding and the aesthetics of your wedding party. While your attire and overall look doesn't have to exactly match with the theme or motif of your wedding, what you wear is ultimately an expression of you, and the details that you wear can be carried throughout the day with colors, textures, and other textiles. Lace details from a wedding gown can be incorporated onto the invitation suite or even delicately piped onto a wedding cake or other confections.

Grooms have so many ways to dress up their style. From cuff links to bow ties, shoes, pocket squares, and cologne, any of these particulars can be stamped with a groom's own mark. As with a bridal suite photo, the thoughtful way a groom puts his look together can be photographed to help document the day with his own panache. By laying out his groom's suite and incorporating details special to him (like a grandfather's watch, father's cuff links, or a friend's borrowed tie), and including details of the wedding, his look can be captured in time.

Incorporating a family member's jewelry is a noted way to tie in heirloom pieces on your wedding day. Whether it's your grandmother's brooch cinched onto the handle of your bouquet, earrings from your fiancé's mother that you wear at the rehearsal dinner, or an entire collection that belongs to your own mother, these pieces can carry sentimental significance.

We always share with our photography partners early on what the details of the morning will look like—what our couples and their wedding parties will be wearing, the getting-ready space, and other details that will become part of the getting-ready photos. This helps to set them up for successfully capturing both bridal and groom "suites" before the wedding.

Work with your photographer to create a collection of your bridal jewelry, along with stationery, your veil, and dress that they can photograph—your perfect style moment will be documented so beautifully by adding in your bouquet or flower buds used in your centerpiece.

Whether you dream of walking down the aisle in simple and sweet ballet flats tied in satin ribbon, barefoot, or in decadent heels studded in jewels, capturing your shoes also becomes part of your wedding style and story. We encourage our brides and grooms to choose elements of style that will be comfortable, first and foremost, and to practice wearing each item to make sure comfort and style are present. Many years ago a sweet bride's gown was altered so tightly that she couldn't sit down at the reception and she nearly passed out—needless to say, she changed mid-reception! Aleah has also sewed many a groom's pants back together after they split on the dance floor! The sign of a great dance party? Yes! But not a good indicator of comfort.

Hair and makeup should be tested in a trial run a couple of months prior to the wedding so you know how your hair will look with your veil and you can gauge the style of makeup and its lasting ability. Think about having your engagement session or another portrait session scheduled on this day so you can actually see how your wedding makeup will look on camera.

Keep in mind that your wedding look should be comfortable and your makeup feel special, but not overdone. You do want to look and feel like yourself, don't you? On the contrary, wedding makeup should be done to last and to stand out in your photos. This is why a hair and makeup trial makes all the difference.

A groom's collection is photographed, capturing the details of his favorite shoes, English cologne, wooden cuff links, and bow tie. This collection becomes the start of his own chapter of the wedding day. A groom's collection of his wedding day accessories is styled "to a T" and laid out on a wooden slab to enhance the feeling of the day.

Camille Wynn, founder of The Dress Theory, adds some additional expert thoughts on finding the dress that best suits you:

Research where *you* want to shop. Most stores cater to a specific style, price range, and environment. Figure out where you want to go, and only go to those shops. There's no need to check out every store in the city or a shop where a coworker got her dress. If you look at stores' Instagram accounts or websites and the aesthetic and prices fit what you're going for, focus on those boutiques first. Brides can get overwhelmed from trying on too many gowns. Most brides feel best visiting just two or three boutiques. Pick your top place or two and go there first. If you've found something you love and can envision yourself getting married in that dress, then it's time to stop. If not, you can book another appointment or two elsewhere if you don't find anything.

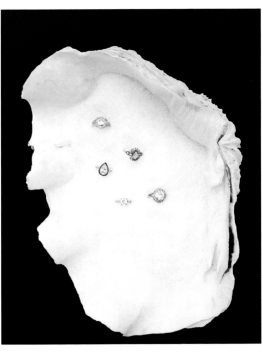

Most brides don't cry, so, it's okay if you don't either. Don't place unrealistic expectations on yourself or your dress. If you love the dress and feel beautiful and excited, it's the one. If you feel like you've found it, stop shopping and start celebrating!

Don't try on dresses that are out of your comfort zone when it comes to pricing. It's not worth it, trust us. If you feel like it could be "the one" and you're comfortable with spending more than expected, go for it. Otherwise, we recommend not trying on gowns that are over your budget unless you've tried everything within your price range and you don't like any. If a stylist pulls out something more expensive without running it by you first, it's definitely okay to tell her you don't want to try it on. Keep in mind, alterations are always needed and they are an additional cost at most boutiques.

Alterations are essential. It's not a place to cut costs. Wedding dress tailoring is truly an art, and a good bridal seamstress is worth the time and money. Tailoring will take a pretty dress from being just pretty and change it into an exquisite gown made for you. It's what makes it YOUR dress!

Limit your party size when gown shopping, if possible. Two to five people is plenty and perfect. If you want to bring more, just know that you may need to tune them out at times to focus on your feelings. And some of your friends may need to share seating depending on the boutique. If you feel like you need a certain person there to help you make your decision, be sure to bring them along or have them ready to FaceTime. Anyone else can always join you at your pickup appointment, accessory styling appointment, or an alterations fitting. It's a great way to make everyone feel included without worrying about their opinions influencing your shopping or experience. Only bring friends or family that you feel you truly need there when you are doing your shopping and decision making.

A few notes about your pre-wedding photography and getting ready:

The strategically planned timing of photography on your wedding day is of high importance to ensure that all of the moments and chapters are captured as you have dreamed them to be. Drafting a wedding day timeline is a big component to your wedding day. A written shared schedule starts the day off on the right foot the morning of the wedding and keeps things flowing along smoothly. Work with your photographer and planner to construct a realistic wedding day timeline to ensure all details are covered. They will also help you plan in some down time in case other elements of the day go off course. Provide your photographer with a list of important details that may not be obvious to them. Tell them about the special earrings you are wearing that were gifted by your fiancé or aunt, the special flower in the bouquets that grew in your grandmother's garden, or components of the meal that represent something original and significant to you. Photographers have a big job in front of them and the more tools they are armed with, the more successfully they can tell your story on camera.

Have your clothing steamed and laid out the night before the wedding. On the morning of your wedding, think about how you want to go into the day—do you and your wedding party have an early morning run planned or will you settle in with mimosas and brunch? How you start the wedding day off can set the tone for your entire day, so thoughtfully plan out how you'd like to spend that early morning time.

Consider who you would like to have with you while you get ready and if you'd like them in robes or fully dressed and ready in the photos. Capturing getting-ready moments of hair and makeup, and everyone getting into their gowns and tuxes generally takes a good hour-and-a-half. Pad extra time into your getting-ready timeline; you don't want to be rushed on your hair and makeup. It's best if the couple is getting ready in nearby locations, as most photographers like to stay together to capture getting-ready details, and this will alleviate photographer travel time.

Before your photographer arrives, find a corner of your getting-ready space to stage your attire—preferably with a window and one that has great natural light. Remember to bring decorative hangers as they will be in the photos. Provide a surface for your photographer to style and photograph accessories on, like a linen from the dining tables or another piece of fabric that coordinates with the wedding day.

Taking a few moments to work with your photographer and mapping out this sacred time will help to ensure a smooth and calm pre-wedding photography schedule.

above: A bouquet of sweet peas cinched up in a navy satin wrap becomes a timeless posy.

above right: A collection of glittering baubles once belonging to a grandmother is on display for a bride to choose from for the big day.

right: Vintage perfume bottles can be displayed for the wedding party to choose their scents on a wedding day.

"I'm not a fan of accessories being photo-graphed in situations that might not actu-ally happen in real life. I don't want to see a stiletto upside down on a palm frond with a wedding ring on the heel. Other than that, anything goes!"

—Alexandra Macon, Co-founder of *Over the Moon* and Weddings Editor at Vogue.com

opposite: Dressing a vintage dress form with a veil can add a sweet touch to a bridal suite, and it also acts as a function in preparation.

above: Family wedding portraits act as a nod to our families, dating back to great-grandparents. A display like this can host touching photos, classic wedding portraits, or even goofy family pictures. Nonetheless, a family photo display is almost always a welcomed idea that guests enjoy.

Personalize It (Favors)

As with most any wedding detail, take-home favors (or parting gifts) are an optional token item that many couples opt to gift to guests as a note of thanks for joining in the celebration. Personalized Frisbee golf discs, bottles of champagne, decadent welcome baskets, personalized cozy blankets, or monogrammed napkins all fall into this category.

Many couples surprise guests with a wedding welcome bag, which often contains an itinerary for the weekend, local sweets and treats, bottled water, and other essentials like sunscreen or bug spray. Featuring jams, candies, and other specialty goods gives your guests a taste of the local flair. Mixing in the heritages or goods from the hometowns of the couple is especially fun and guests will enjoy tasting local taffy, ketchup potato chips, or other quirky or amusing treats that speak to the region or come from your favorite bakery. Some couples choose to forego favors, which is acceptable as well, but we do love a good takeaway. They can be an exciting and even eccentric gift that your guests will rave about if it tells your story.

The presentation for these ideas can lend a great opportunity to add another scene or experience to your wedding. Your wait staff can pass out favors on gold trays, guests can help themselves to favors staged on a beautiful table or piece of furniture, or you can pass out your favors yourselves as you visit each dining table during dinner. The idea of wedding favors, no matter how ornate or simple, is simply a way of giving thanks and leaving that extra lasting impression on your guests when they depart your soirée and head home.

oppostie: Boxed sea salted caramels from Fran's Chocolates in Seattle are stacked and displayed on gold mirrored trays from Aleah's grandmother, mimicking a wedding cake. They can be served as a bite-sized dessert or as take-home gifts at night's end.

left: Clever paper butterflies with guests' names scrolled with table numbers instantly become an interactive display indicating at which dining table they'll be seated.

"When it comes to welcome bags, my new favorite idea is to include a deck of cards by Peep's Paper Products. They can be customized to reflect your tastes and preferences, and you can include fun, whimsical illustrations of items that have meaning to you and your future spouse on the cards. These are a cute way to set the mood for the weekend, but they're also something the couple and their guests can use down the line. They'll forever serve as a reminder of this special day."

—Alexandra Macon

opposite: If you have ever been to a Valley & Company event, chances are you have a soft shawl given to you on a tray, carefully wrapped in silk ribbon. Such an easy presentation, but we can't tell you how many ladies at our weddings are beyond delighted when we hand them one of these.

Clockwise, beginning upper left corner: Fresh berry boxes make great to-go treats; wooden boxes filled with local bounty create a welcoming gift for guests; potted herbs host calligraphy escort cards; hand-written calligraphy tags create a fluttering escort card display in an orchard; a big basket filled with citrus welcomes guests at the entry, and hand-penned leaves indicate guests' names and table numbers; French violet candies presented in vellum envelopes are sweet and pretty.

Cocktail Hour & After Party

At more and more of our weddings our clients are requesting
a pre-ceremony "happy hour," where guests are greeted
with either a cocktail, glass of champagne, or water station.
In the summer months, a lemonade stand, with options
for adding muddled blackberries or rosemary, can be a
nostalgic and elevated treat. For a winter wedding, a warm
apple cider will do the trick. At some weddings we offer
pre-ceremony bites like popcorn in printed bags, cookies,
Popsicles, or other appetizers, especially if we know
most guests are traveling a distance for the festivities.

Welcoming guests is of high importance to us, and we also know that at more weddings than not, guests show up early, so why not give them an unexpected treat before the ceremony? While this notion might not work at a church ceremony, it fares well for private homes or venues where it is timeline and layout appropriate. For a glitzy New Year's Eve wedding we welcomed guests in from the chilly night air before the ceremony with an espresso and biscotti cart. It was an unexpected, sweet way for them to be greeted—not to mention, it was very Seattle.

Waiters have served caviar or oysters on the half shell for our events, shucked on the spot, and servers have passed out champagne with edible gold flecks. Guests have eaten Chinese food in takeout boxes, street tacos cooked on the spot, and epic raw seafood bars that rival the best restaurants' displays. Your happy hour can be as over-the-top or as minimalist as you like. Just remember that the influences of you are what will make it special.

Traditionally, the time between a ceremony and reception is treated as "cocktail hour," or "happy hour," as we like to call it. Post-ceremony guests may head to the bar for drinks, hug friends and family they haven't seen in some time, kiss and congratulate the newlyweds, sign the guest book, sample hors d'oeuvres, and just relax and enjoy the setting. This time can be logistically important behind-the-scenes, as catering and planning teams may flip a room, light candles, set up seating displays, and add last-minute touches before a reception begins and guests are seated for the next scene. Depending on your guest count, this time can be as short as thirty minutes for smaller numbers, or up to ninety minutes for weddings with

A cozy sofa and chair create an intimate nook to enjoy champagne and conversation. Add beautiful roses to the mix and you have instant charm.

more than two hundred guests, as it takes a good deal more time to usher and filter guests through a layout. Happy hour is also an excellent time to give your timeline a bit of padding in case things earlier in the day or at the ceremony slip off track a bit.

Happy hour is where your favorite cocktails and spirits are served, guests can play games, visit, and just enjoy the sights, sounds, and tastes of your wedding. We love to recommend activity-driven components like wood-fired pizzas made to order, wine tasting and food pairings, tequila flights, lawn games, a caricature artist, upbeat music, and other interactive happenings that will delight guests and leave a lasting impression. This time becomes a warm-up for the fun of your wedding to come.

It is also a critical time to have ample seating and places to go for your guests. Staging a dozen cocktail tables in varying sizes with other soft seating and coffee tables or big trunks may feel like furniture excess, but during this time guests really want to just park and enjoy the surroundings, and it's often where guests get their wedding "bearings"—they make themselves at home, find the restrooms, find their escort cards, and grab their food and drink and kick back. Renting lounge furniture and creating intentional vignettes for guests to experience will not only look lovely, but it will provide that level of comfort you want to create. Adding a handful of festive patio umbrellas to the mix can add to your décor and also provide that much-needed shade from the sun in the summer months. Finally, staging a few patio heaters can never hurt. Even on the hottest of days, nights can turn a bit chilly no matter where you live. Use our

mantra of creating a totally unexpected setting for your cocktail hour that has an abundance of character. Regardless of how simplified or extravagant your activities and food and drink are, you have every excuse to indulge in a festive cocktail hour!

If all that wasn't celebration enough, have you ever experienced an after-party at a wedding you attended? We are seeing more couples wanting to create a post-wedding shindig, which becomes a separate moment in time with a different energy and look all to itself. We find that after-parties are for the late-night crowd who are generally peers of the couple. It's a way of keeping the party moving and taking advantage of having friends all in one place one last time. After-parties can take place at a totally different venue, with a change of attire for the guests. It can be a bonfire with s'mores and beer where guests just hang out in jeans and relax on the beach, or it can take be an impromptu gathering of wedding guests in the hotel lobby or at a nearby tavern. Some of our favorite after-parties are where the entire wedding party in their wedding attire or in ball gowns and tuxes all gather at the couple's favorite dive bar. The after-party is a continuation of the festivities and, as you guessed it, another way to gather with your guests and to close out your wedding story. You can simply corral the last revelers at your wedding and all casually caravan to your favorite local spot, or make a reservation in advance where you pre-pay for drinks and order a few dozen appetizers like sliders, mac and cheese, French fries, crab cakes, or even chips and guacamole and salsa to be served when you arrive. Think of this segment as its own little event and remember that it can be as formal and planned or as impromptu as you wish!

We almost always recommend that our couples have at least two bars at their wedding, especially for a larger guest count. Consider one a satellite bar, where beer, wine, and sparkling water is pre-poured and ready for easy access, and the other a specialty bar where your fanciful cocktails are served up. Think about ways to alleviate lines and guest waiting time, and this is generally where to start. Your satellite bar can be closed once happy hour is completed, but it will help your bartenders as well as speed up the drink service.

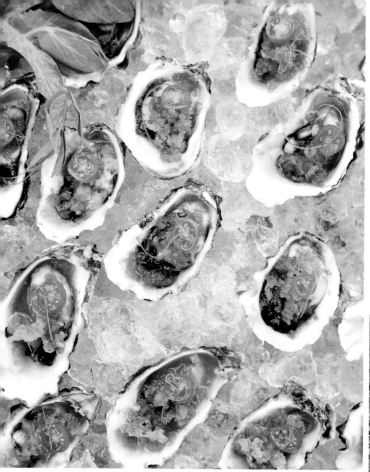

opposite: A large wooden bar hosts glasses ready to be served to guests and acts as a happy hour focal point. This bar acts as another surface for a bountiful arrangement as well!

left: Local oysters served on the half shell with Bloody Mary ice are not only pretty to look at, but refreshing to eat.

below left: Fried chicken and champagne from Lisa Dupar Catering provide a touch of Southern hospitality with an unexpected twist.

below: Leather chairs from Found Vintage Rentals provide an intimate and shady place for guests to share in a conversation. They also add to the décor and ambiance of the wedding.

Cocktails can truly be works of art and their presentation exquisite, especially when served with accoutrements like herbs, crushed ice, beautiful edible flowers, and citrus peels.

Here are some delightful cocktails from Perfect Pour Cocktail Co.:

Bramble in the Bronx

1½ ounces Big Gin
½ ounce blackberry shrub
1½ ounces lemon cordial

Shake all ingredients with ice and pour into a chilled glass.

Fleur de Lis

1¼ ounces Big Gin
½ ounce crème de violette
½ ounce lemon
½ ounce honey-lavender syrup
1 egg white
1½ ounces Prosecco
Teapot Bitters

Shake all ingredients except the Prosecco and Teapot Bitters with ice for 20 seconds, and then strain and shake again for 20 seconds without ice. Add Prosecco and pour into a couple of martini glasses. Spritz the Bitters over the cocktail. Garnish with a lavender sprig.

Mai Tai

½ ounce macadamia nut orgeat
¼ ounce falernum
1 ounce lime
½ ounce Pierre Ferrand Dry Curaçao
1½ ounces Appleton Estates 12-year Jamaican Rum
½ ounce Byrrh Quinquina Wine
Smith & Cross Overproof Jamaican Rum

Shake all ingredients except the Quinine Wine and Smith & Cross. Strain over crushed ice and top with the Byrrh. Mist some Smith & Cross over the top of the cocktail. Garnish with an Amarena cherry and a mint sprig.

Wedding Desserts

The great fun about choosing your wedding dessert is that
it truly can be anything that your sweet tooth craves—
you may not even like sweets! Over the years guests have
enjoyed after-dinner fruit platters paired with cream,
shortcakes stacked with stone fruit or berries, decadent
chocolate bars, an espresso and biscotti cart, Popsicles, and
virtually everything in between! When it comes to deciding
what to serve your guests after dinner, the possibilities
are nearly limitless. This scene of your wedding is a
wonderful way to incorporate something totally traditional
or absolutely unexpected that's in line with your story.
Some couples choose to serve dessert as a first course (yes,
please!). You may opt for the tradition of wedding cake
and a cake cutting ceremony, which we cherish as well.

esserts can be presented as stations or buffets, served family style to dining tables on platters, or created as a singular wow factor in the middle of a tent or reception room on a table of its own near the dance floor dressed with candles and flowers. Ice cream can be scooped and served from a bicycle cart, and doughnuts can be fried up and sprinkled with toppings on site, hot and fresh! Truly, the idea of a wedding dessert can be translated in so many creative ways. Consider the timing of your desserts and how long the ceremony of serving that dessert will take—desserts like chocolates or macarons set on table could mean guests are welcome to graze all evening, whereas a traditional wedding cake that is served and passed out to each guest during toasting will be enjoyed and guests can move on to the next scene.

Use this time to serve guests food and drinks that you both love and that you're excited to show off. This menu can be as indulgent and layered or as simple and perfectly delicious as you prefer. With desserts, a stunning and fun presentation will only enhance the experience.

opposite: A whimsical floral-inspired cake takes on a majestic feeling when staged near a thicket atop a botanical print linen.

above: An heirloom cake cutting set passed down from a grandmother is used as a ceremonial honor during cake cutting.

Clockwise, beginning upper left corner: Wedding pies are so much fun to serve, especially when guests can choose from an assortment of flavors. Serve pies à la mode with a big scoop of your favorite flavors; little vanilla sandwich cookies are a great tasty bite and favor; mini cheese cakes consist of small wheels of goat cheese and soft French cheeses and are topped with berries. Serve these at each dining table along with honey and herbed crackers for an unexpected treat with a bit of European flair; doughnuts—always a welcomed treat! Dozens of doughnuts, displayed on chic marble stands, become an instant favorite treat. Maple bars, old-fashioned doughnuts, sprinkled doughnuts, or even doughnut holes are all unusual to serve but oh-so welcome; a sweets table created by Tallant House displayed decadent treats like mini cheesecakes, bars, and fruit tarts for a summertime soirée.

above: This three-tiered white cake is dressed with black-berry vines and fresh, plump berries, sitting on top of a black Mosser Glass stand.

right: Talk about a statement piece: this seven-tiered tow-ering cake is elegant and classic and subtly dressed with delicate piping and the couple's monogram.

above left: Popsicles are an unexpected treat for guests when served on a Popsicle cart or passed on demi plates.

above right: Macarons, when stacked on small cake stands, become edible art that guests can nibble on.

right: Cake slices are truly works of art, especially when served to guests at their dining table on modern white plates.

above: Cookies can be a fun take-home at the end of the evening (hand them out with individual cartons of milk!).

Receptions/Place Settings

No matter how ornate and wild, or as understated or classic you dream of your wedding looking and feeling, simple components really do translate throughout. Every table begins with a base and can be altered to create the look you envision. A neutral base of linen; decorative—yet smart—flatware; a white plate; three goblets for red wine, white wine, and water; and a white linen hemstitch napkin can set a pretty base. Adding to or enhancing this sample place setting can be done by swapping out linens for an ornate patterned fabric or one with a velvety texture, using a gauzy runner, incorporating taper candles or short votives, and adding layers with a place card, a menu, or a thank-you note set atop the place setting. A wedding favor, loose fruit, and scattered blooms can only enhance a place setting.

hether you dream up over-the-top centerpieces that dance above guests' heads, understated and low flowers that allow for great conversation, or include the minimal settings you need for service, keep in mind that place settings should ultimately be comfortable for your guests and, of course, represent you. Consider staging a mock-up with your designer or planner to see what a place setting will look and feel like to ensure enough elbow room, conversation room, and space for flatware, china, glassware, candles, and other accoutrements you choose to place.

Music Style

We often refer to the moments of a wedding day as scenes
when we're planning the day's festivities with our clients.
These scenes are broadly (but commonly) broken out into
1) the guests arrival prior to the ceremony, 2) the ceremony
itself, 3) the post-ceremony (happy hour), 4) dinner
festivities, and 5) dancing and merriment—the party!

usic can play a large role in the structure for each scene as it can immediately set the tempo for each moment. Think about the feeling and the movement that you envision for each of your scenes; do you close your eyes and see a lively ceremony that's nontraditional or do you dream of walking down the aisle to a classic string quartet? Do you want your dinnertime music to feel jazzy and nostalgic or unexpected and new age?

Sit down with a pen and paper and focus solely on the sounds that you want your guests to hear throughout each scene. Be sure to include your favorite songs throughout.

What can be so fun about the music planning is that there really are no rules (or there shouldn't be). Thinking creatively can only help tie in your story. In past weddings we have surprised guests with a bagpiper who seemingly appeared out of nowhere, staged live Polynesian music and luau lessons during a formal dinner, and seen every style of music played from Chilean guitar to jazz, live music to DJs, quartets, soloists, and impromptu singers. The possibilities for exceptional music can truly enhance the memories from your wedding day.

opposite: Patricio Contreras, an incredible Chilean guitarist, plays for guests before the ceremony begins and through cocktail hour. His lively talents are versatile and become a beautiful backdrop for conversation.

above: The Chris Friel Orchestra, a live Seattle-area band, sets the tempo for an unforgettable dance party.

designs

Inspiration can truly be found anywhere—from a favorite restaurant's motif to beautiful architecture during travels abroad, a neighbor's flourishing garden that seamlessly changes with the seasons, or family traditions passed down from great-grandparents to present-day children. Such inspiration has a way of finding you, oftentimes when you least expect it.

When dreaming up your own wedding vision, aim at finding a balance of ingredients that tie into your own story and history with design elements that speak to you. Whether it's a colorful signature cocktail, a special appetizer that nods to your favorite meal, flowers that you exchanged on your fifth date, or colors that remind you both of that sunset on your tropical vacation together, your storied wedding can start to take shape by finding inspiration, whether you're actively seeking it or by it jumping out at you when you least expect it.

While there is no perfect recipe for a wedding, we hope that you find an inspiring combination of ceremony styles, table layouts and settings, color pairings, flower inspiration, and the like within these pages. Put your own stamp on the bits and pieces you pull from the following designs and weddings.

Details needn't be overdone or underdone. They should look and feel exactly like you want them to. The experiences that you create for you and your guests should feel comfortable and happy.

When we talk about design, we are discussing the entire work of art of your wedding, from the flowers and linens to the stationery, the sounds guests will hear, the smells, the food and drink, and the scenes. We look at each event as if it's a play, with each segment of the day being considered a scene. We plan the details of each scene thoughtfully, through creative timing, guest movement, and by peppering in experiences throughout every scene. Each scene should build up to the culmination of an incredible reception.

Starting to plan the scenes of your day can begin with the feelings you want your guests to experience when they enter your wedding and when they leave. Some couples tell us they dream of guests feeling welcomed and cozy. We may create some kind of welcome station at this wedding, where guests are greeted with a warm cocktail or mocktail before the ceremony and a shawl cinched in ribbon. For other couples who want their guests to enter their celebration being blown away, we would kick off the festivities with a bang, instead of building up to the wow crescendo. We might usher guests into a pre-ceremony happy hour with fabulous draping and lighting, a lively band, and a towering champagne presentation.

Think about the feelings you want to evoke at your wedding. This exercise will help you to achieve those feelings throughout each scene. Presentation is a key in helping you to create your own story—no matter how simplified or elaborate.

There is something to be said about how designs are presented and how designs can add to the memories of a wedding.

Anna Price Olson, Real Weddings Editor at *BRIDES*, shares some excellent
and creative ideas for personalization:

A couple can use their personal style to tell their story, first and foremost, with fashion. I love it when a bride tells me that her dress reflects her everyday style. Obviously, it's not always a one-to-one translation, but if you wear clean lines and crisp silhouettes to work daily, that can absolutely translate to a modern, structured wedding dress. And the same goes with the groom's attire. I'm seeing more and more guys create custom suits with a hand-selected color, cut, or sometimes even a fun monogram or fabric on the inside. Beyond fashion, I think it's unique when a couple brings a bit of their personal style to the décor as well. When creating a design scheme and color palette, it's smart to look to what you like on an everyday basis. (Who do you follow on Instagram? What photos do you like? How have you decorated your home?) This can influence your wedding décor—and make it unique to you! For example, if your apartment is filled with succulents, think about using those on your reception tables instead of abundant arrangements of peonies. We even had a couple re-create their exact dining-room table for the head table!

I get so excited when I see a personalized idea I've never seen before. A recent favorite is a monogrammed cocktail. We featured a wedding on BRIDES.com where the couple had their bartender create their wedding crest (their last initials entwined) in the foam on top of the drink, which they served in a pretty coupe glass. Another was simply adding special stamps to the outside envelope of their invitation. The couple lives in D.C., so they did a stamp with the U.S. capitol on it, one from the groom's hometown, one from the state of their destination wedding, and another from the bride's alma mater. It was a simple twist on something they already needed, but it made the suite so beautiful and told a bit about the couple's story as well. One bride and groom hired an illustrator to draw a map of their destination-wedding location—as you often see in the invite suite or on a couple's wedding website—and then printed it on large white beach towels (since it was a beach location) as a personalized welcome gift. Beyond putting your twist on the day's details, it's also fun to think about your guests. We featured a wedding where the couple had an illustrator draw pictures of every single guest for their escort cards. I can only imagine how fun it was to find your seat—and take home a picture at the end of the night!

Garden Charm

The notion of a garden-style wedding is one that evokes
a sense of romantic nostalgia and also a timeless charm.
We dreamed up this setting with the thought in mind of
a wedding party gathering al fresco—surrounded by lush
flowers that sing, delicious yet unpretentious food that can be
shared family-style, and a bridal style kissed with traditional
elements like antique lace, a family heirloom diamond ring, a
velvet-lined ring box, and a playful bouquet rich in color and
texture, paired with a delicate gold headpiece perfectly fitting
to a garden bride's spirited style.

A garden wedding can take place at home, at a venue with sprawling grounds, or a public park. Elements from a garden-style wedding can be incorporated into virtually any style of property through table settings, overhead flower installations, linens, and stationery. Think about creating tucked-away areas as you would find in a rambling garden with wonderful details hidden around each corner of your venue—use trailing vines to dress up a dessert table or a playful patterned floral linen to host your wedding cake. Stage an interactive salmon grilling station with a sparkling wine pairing in a corner of the space, or have a friendly cheese monger explain types of cheese, fruits, preserves, and nuts to guests in another focal area.

Jacin Fitzgerald, founder of Jacin Fitzgerald Events, shares some
of her creative thoughts on personalized details and flowers:

Anything out of the box, or not yet on Pinterest, is sure to be memorable, but personalization is also key in creating an event for the books. Pulling in those sentimental details, perhaps your grandmother's favorite flower or a nod to your shared alma mater, or maybe incorporating your pet in your wedding crest, will make your guests feel as though they participated in something truly special. Timeless wedding design isn't about going over the top, it's about paying attention to the details that matter most, and the more personalized these may be, the more memorable the overall experience becomes.

Color trends seem to come and go, and it seems as though the time-honored traditions such as tossing the bouquet or garter are more popular some years than others, but I think something old, new, borrowed, and blue has been consistent through it all. This is an opportunity for a bride to incorporate heirlooms into her big day, whether it's repurposing her mother's veil or sewing her grandfather's handkerchief into her gown. Though it's such a tiny component in the grand scheme of wedding planning, it is one of the traditions that carries on for generations to come and evokes a feeling of nostalgia far beyond the big day.

You can always tuck a favorite bloom into a bouquet or boutonnière, but sometimes the flowers may not match or may have a hard time lasting through the day. We had a bride whose late grandmother loved gardenias (a flower with the most beautiful scent but known to brown quickly if over-handled), so we tucked hundreds of them into the ceremony arch. You could see a few peeking out, but more important, the beautiful perfume filled the air reaching those who knew of Grandma's affection for this special bloom. Another option is through the paper goods, incorporating sentimental flowers into the wedding stationery or crest, to give them a new life on paper.

opposite left: A painterly wedding invitation indicates to guests that a charming celebration lies ahead, complete with a hand-painted envelope liner and layered look. The artistic charm of a hand-painted invitation tells guests early on that a thoughtful wedding has been planned.

opposite right: A tucked away surprise, a canopy of wisteria sets the tone for a stately and enchanting garden setting.

Greeting guests with a refreshment is a welcomed token. Your welcome drinks can be alcoholic
or non- and we suggest staging a cart or table with
pour-yourself water, infused with citrus, berries,
or mint. Especially in warm summertime months,
this station will be welcomed.

above left: These berry spritzers, made with muddled blackberries and topped with champagne, are a beautiful tie-in to
the natural garden setting.

above right: Handmade lanterns romantically illuminate the
pathway through the woods, leaving a mark of enchantment
for departing guests.

right: For the ceremony setting, we wanted to create
something intimate, yet lush and, well, garden inspired. We
adorned a cathedral-style arch with layers of greenery, starting with bay leaves, salal sprigs, asparagus and ladder ferns,
and colorful flowers.

A luscious cascading bouquet is filled with dozens of garden roses, scabiosa, berry-hued yarrow, and bay leaves. The bouquet has a loose and flowing structure that creates a plucked-from-the-garden look.

To make this bouquet:

12 branches of bay

12 stems of deep scabiosa

10 stems of cream garden rose

10 stems of blush garden rose

20 stems of Distant Drum garden roses

10 branches of raspberry on the vine

above left: A glittering antique diamond ring is presented in a moss-filled glass hexagon in a vintage ring box. Presentation on a wedding day is of the utmost importance when talking about the details, and creating a special setting for a ring to be staged is not only extra special, but when captured on camera, creates an heirloom photo.

above right: A decadent cheese and fruit display can be a welcomed dessert or a pre-dessert treat when presented to dining tables.

above: This wedding cake looks like it belongs at a garden wedding, doesn't it? The detail of the hand-sculpted flowers and the delicate greenery make it a romantic statement all its own.

opposite top left: Blueberry branches were carefully placed on top of each place setting—a simple, yet thoughtful finishing touch that looks breathtaking when replicated on each napkin.

opposite top right: Fresh berries lend a sweet and edible accent to the tabletop, and an extra special sentiment when presented in family cut-crystal dessert cups. Such items nod to a couple's love of blueberry pie and late summer berry picking.

opposite bottom: Marzipan treats cinched in small muslin bags stamped with a wax seal are a thoughtful parting favor.

Something Blue

The saying goes something old, something new,
something borrowed, something blue . . . This particular
shade of blue was ever-present in our own wedding,
and has a cameo in our company's logo. It's a sweet and
refreshing hue that to us represents not only our own
story, but the classic wedding phrase.

This something blue setting was inspired by subtle ocean waves and crystal-clear glass, suggesting a timeless setting anchored by billowing blue fabrics flanking the sailcloth tent and gauzy table runners dancing across crisp, white Swiss dot linens. We dreamed of creating a private setting surrounded by a woodsy environment, like many of our private home or estate weddings.

Whether you are hosting several hundred of your closest friends and family or an intimate gathering of a dozen, a tented wedding can feel so intimate and welcoming. It can be dressed up or down with greenery garlands, fabric pole covers, lighting (like bistro lights or up-lights), and with virtually any kind of seating configuration. In a vast open space, a tent can give a sense of definition and place for your guests to get comfortable for the night. A small sailcloth tent can be utilized for a lounge or dancing tent or as a stand-alone bar and landing point for guests to sit back and enjoy their cocktails while watching the bustle of the evening unfold.

opposite: A decorative pale blue wedding cake created by Lilac Cake Boutique sat atop its own small round table, creating an added focal point under the cozy tent.

above left: Monogrammed napkins are fitting for post-ceremony festivities and are a charming way for a couple to showcase their personalized style. The couple can use these napkins in their new home to entertain, or for every day.

above right: Mix and match clean details like crisp white linens and plates with antique silver to create an unexpected interest.

above: A champagne tower stacked with coupes makes an exciting conversation piece for guests.

opposite: The bridal bouquet hosts shade-loving hostas, periwinkle hydrangea, bear grass, snow-on-the-mountain, and white peonies—clean and understated.

Old-World Romance

The old stone buildings at Whetstone Wine Cellars in Napa became the perfect setting for this old-world wedding. The sentiment behind an old-world-inspired celebration is one that is of the highest quality and thought. Old-world elements are those that have stellar craftsmanship and history—and an old-world venue is one that is steeped in stories itself.

Intricate lace, a cathedral veil, velvet linens, breezy fabrics, and luscious flowers and vines came together to create this timeless and utterly enchanting display. A tall wall, deep-rooted with vines, made for an everlasting ambiance that felt both cozy as well as dramatic. When dreaming up a location for your wedding reception, look to a space that has a natural backdrop for your setting, one that will enhance your designs.

A creative assortment of textures (candlesticks, glassware, patterned flatware, and a table runner) combined on a tabletop created a styled, layered look. The use of velvet linens enriched the table setting and the cut crystal stemware provided that added polish and formality to the scene.

above: A cathedral veil brings a dramatic romance to the ceremony and can be removed before the reception begins.

opposite: The illustration of the property became an instant keepsake in the invitation suite.

This arched bridge created a picture-perfect location for a timeless bridal portrait.

opposite top left: Champagne flutes are elevated when passed with rose petals surrounding the stems.

opposite top right: A sporty vintage getaway car is dressed with greenery and flowers, signifying the perfect grand exit.

opposite bottom left: A crystal punch bowl housing flowers is not only an unusual vessel for a centerpiece, but it becomes a conversation piece and a wedding keepsake.

opposite bottom right: Sweet flowers and greens like scented geranium leaves create a charming wreath to welcome guests.

Napa Winery

Winery weddings tend to bring a sense of openness and a family feeling. There can also be a feeling of structure from the long rows of growing grapevines. These weddings carry a great charm and can be dressed up or down, enhancing the setting and playing off the natural colors of the surroundings. We incorporate touches of vineyards thoughtfully, starting with the invitation that may nod to grapes or grape leaves, and carry these subtle details throughout, like placing vines around napkins, grape clusters nestled among the vines or greenery runners down a tabletop, or through an illustration of a winery that we carry through with cocktail napkins or paper goods.

This setting in Napa called for us to mimic the gorgeous natural surroundings and colors. We painted the design with muted mustard, a soft plum, pale orange, wooded brown, and natural greens and incorporated all of these colors into the tabletop and place settings. Terracotta vessels hosted flickering tea lights and our luscious centerpieces, and tiny vines were wrapped around the napkins, as if they were a little gift welcoming guests to their place settings.

To capture the nature of the setting, stand-alone photos of the vineyards were taken, becoming works of art on their own.

opposite: An over-sized bouquet hosts roses, oak leaves, pieris, and elements that complement the vineyard setting.

below left: Freshly baked breads are passed around family-style.

below right: We made our mustard napkins and cinched them with delicate vines to add a bit of vineyard sweetness.

above left: Local fresh bounty is served tableside for dinner.

above right: Figs and grapes act as décor when staggered down the table and in terra-cotta pots, but they also help to tell the story of the winery setting.

left: Copper bells became a sweet wedding favor.

opposite: A vintage roadster is at the ready for a grand exit.

Estate

Whether you or your family call a quaint cabin in the mountains, a sprawling beachside property, or the house you grew up in in the city your home, getting married there can be an incredibly special moment at a place already steeped in memories. We were married at the island home of Aleah's parents, where decades of memories had been made and captured. It gave us a truly blank canvas to plan and design our own nuptials around—no one had ever been married there before—and still holds a special place in our hearts.

Blackberry vines, tea roses, cupcake cosmos, and mint
seemingly grow out of tall white vessels.

Over the years we have taken part in tapping into many fun family traditions for our clients at their homes, like ringing a dinner bell to call guests to happy hour, shooting off a cannon (Nick loved this!) after our couple said we do, and observing tried and true traditions that were of high importance to our couples and their families.

While private residences can allow for multiple opportunities for layouts and scenes, aim to keep guests central and gathered together so you don't lose momentum. When planning an estate wedding, think about how to enhance the natural spaces like garden scenery, a bluff overlooking the water, or a long and dramatic winding driveway. How can you put a wedding twist on those areas that some guests may have seen before? Staging your guest book in an herb garden, illuminating that long pathway with a hundred candles or dozens of lanterns, or lighting up the house with dramatic professional lighting are all ways to put a wedding spin on the home.

opposite: Masculine details like the groom's grandfather's antique binoculars, watch, and barometer help set the tone for the groom's suite.

above: Mint and clover added texture and a lushness to these centerpieces in a modern white vessel.

left: Emerald jewels make for an heirloom bridal photo when styled with a crystal perfume bottle and antique hydrangea.

opposite: A decadent cake balances stately details like a worn leather finish, gold brushing, and black almost Art Deco-feeling diamonds hand cut to bring a sense of balance. Hand-modeled flowers top the cake.

Modern

A modern wedding can stand for endless designs and styles. To us it means a stately look that could take place on a number of stages—quite literally—but also in a studio space, a museum, or at a chic restaurant. We designed something a bit moodier by incorporating onyx ghost chairs and darker stationery, but still kept the setting light with crisp white linens, plates, and ethereal flowers with a botanical specimen touch. Modern can often start with clean lines and a blocked base and be built up with more flourishing details.

The clean lines can start with the base of your tables, the outline of your chairs, and even the type of vessels that your centerpieces will be held in. Think sharp and sleek, like tall acrylic stands to host flowers at the altar, or black flatware with no detailing. For a modern wedding, an open floor plan with room for your party to flow will always suit a design goal. Use accent tones (like a rich plum and a deep forest green) to bring a balance and sense of interest to your overall design, your tabletop, and details like stationery and place settings.

Small square wooden plates were set atop the table with stacks of fresh figs to snack on, lending to the décor and ambiance.

opposite top, left to right: This wedding invitation lends that unexpected botanical air with a printed clematis envelope liner and a fanciful font; in the tradition of telling your story, why not serve guests your favorite biscotti and wine for dessert? It brings a feeling of an intimate dinner party.

opposite bottom, left to right: Simple taper candles cinched in black ribbon turned into creative party favors; glittering diamond earrings and an engagement ring are perched atop a scented geranium posy.

above: Tall black taper candles stand in clear glass holders, adding some romantic drama to the table and carrying the deep onyx tone throughout.

opposite: The geometric, squared-off cake sings modern, but is softened with delicate monochromatic white detailing.

real weddings

*Each of these celebrations tells their own spectacular story—
from the style of stationery and invitations created from scratch
to the color palette each couple carefully chose, to the style of
music compiled, the look of the wedding party, the luscious
flowers, and what their guests ate and drank. Each wedding is
totally unique and perfectly them. We are thrilled to share each
of these special weddings and their original stories from our
couples, as well as some fun insider planning ideas including
their actual menus and the components of their bouquets and
boutonnières.*

Ashley & Max

Bohemian Estate Wedding

Ashley and Max's wedding planning took place in about four months—not an unusual feat for us, but about eight months shorter than our average lead time. It just meant that we put our getting to know each other time into high gear! The wedding took place in the beautiful woodsy home where Ashley grew up, which gave us the flexibility to create a seamless and pretty magical layered wedding with experiences and fun transitions around each corner.

During the wedding planning time, we got to know Ashley and Max rather quickly but very well, understanding their desire for an incredible party where their guests (who would be traveling from San Diego and elsewhere) would feel welcomed and well taken care of from the moment they stepped onto the scenic forested grounds of the property.

One of the special moments of the day was when both Ashley and Max's parents stood on the bridge and greeted all of the guests as they meandered down to the ceremony, while an attentive welcome staff passed out champagne. What a memorable sentiment and also a great introduction for new family. It is this kind of personal touch that creates a lasting memory for guests.

Ashley's bouquet was a beautiful arrangement of white foxglove, white hydrangea, nine bark, ferns, and white stock.

Max's boutonnière was created with white sweetheart roses, and grape leaves.

Ashley's style was romantic with some bohemian infusion—her bridal style was ethereal and dreamy. The special touches we created that day nodded to that—gorgeous greenery, native flowers and plants, antique sideboards to house the berry-laden cake, eclectic furniture for guests to lounge on, crystal chandeliers suspended in trees, and a sailcloth tent to house it all. Their menu catered to both Ashley's native Pacific Northwest, with oyster shooters and local cheeses, and Max's hometown of San Diego, with incredible gourmet street tacos.

Ashley and her brother grew up around animals and, while the corral on the property no longer houses any animals, we brought in a menagerie of farm animals to add some excitement to the corrals surrounding the dining tent, and to bring that bit of nostalgia back to the grounds.

A striking white horse, a short and stout salt-and-peppered pony, a majestic chestnut stallion, and goats rounded out our woodsy zoo. We even temporarily named the two goats Hugo and Clyde and gave them greenery necklaces—which didn't last long before they were nibbled off! It's this kind of touch that becomes so unexpected and offers a layer to a wedding story.

For the dinner set up for the reception, guests were invited into the greenery-cloaked tent for dinner but were encouraged to mix and mingle at small bistro-sized tables, larger family-style tables, cocktail tables, and on sofas and pews. Ashley and Max wanted their guests to experience a more casual atmosphere for dinner rather than a long and formal sit-down meal, so this style of dining was warm and welcoming.

What they ate and drank

Dinner: A Taste of Washington

Arugula and grilled peaches—compressed and grilled peaches, shaved pecorino, and balsamic glaze

Charred broccolini with Marcona almonds with garlic, lemon, and olive oil

Smoked salmon with lemon caper dill aioli sauce

House artisan bread with Sonoma sea salt butter

San Diego Samplers

"Build your own" So Cal street tacos— carne asada, camerones a la diabla, New Mexico chili grilled chicken served on handmade corn tortillas, topped with guest's choice of pico de gallo

"Dirty corn"—grilled summer corn, scallion butter, chili-lime aioli, cotija cheese, and cilantro pesto

Something Sweet

Stacked carrot cake

Sea salted caramels

Libation Offerings

Max's San Diego Margarita

Ash's NW sparkling berry lemonade

Assorted vodka, tequila, gin, and whiskey cocktails

Wine, bubbly, and beer

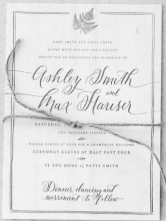

Greg Smith and Patty Smith
ALONG WITH JOE AND FRED HAUSER
INVITE YOU TO CELEBRATE THE MARRIAGE OF

Ashley Smith
and
Max Hauser

SATURDAY, THE
TWO THOUSAND SIXTEEN

PLEASE ARRIVE AT FOUR FOR A CHAMPAGNE WELCOME
CEREMONY BEGINS AT HALF PAST FOUR

AT THE HOME of PATTY SMITH

*Dinner, dancing and
merriment to follow*

PLEASE DELIVER TO:

514 Gerard Ave No.
La Jolla California
92037

Join Us!

M _____

_____ ACCEPTS WITH PLEASURE

_____ NUMBER ATTENDING

_____ DECLINES WITH REGRET

Kindly
RESPOND BY AUGUST 15

Valley & Co.
Seattle, Washington
98103

Details

ACCOMMODATIONS

There are a number of AirBnB properties and hotels
in nearby Issaquah or Snoqualmie.

VENUE DETAILS

This wedding and all of the festivities will take place outdoors
so we encourage ladies to wear comfortable flats or wedges.
Please bring a shawl for the evening.

There is no parking available on property. Please plan on
alternative transportation, such as Uber or a taxi service.

CHILDREN

We love your kiddos but this is an adults only evening.
We hope this evening out means you are still able to share
our big day and will enjoy having the evening off!

FOR MORE INFORMATION

www.ashleyandmax.com

Welcome
TO THE PARTY!
PLEASE FIND A SEAT, GRAB A PLATE AND CELEBRATE!

enjoy the evening!

Ashley recalls the favorite parts of her wedding day:

Max and I live in La Jolla, which is where Max grew up. Since we were getting married at my mom's home in Sammamish, we wanted to be sure to incorporate aspects of Max's hometown, too. We had two catering stations: a Pacific Northwest station featuring local salmon and veggies, and a San Diego station featuring delicious street tacos. It was relaxed and fun—exactly what we were hoping for. We had a blast dancing together and a bunch of us finished the night off with some late night swimming in my mom's pool.

Getting married in the woods I grew up in was magical—it's one of my favorite places in the world. We even got to take pictures in my childhood tree fort! All the animals in the pasture had these darling floral collars Valley & Co. made for them. So cute!

I loved my dress. It was nontraditional and not at all what I pictured myself ever getting married in—but it was perfect for the day. I wanted to feel comfortable (which was why I opted for flats) but still elegant—and not (completely) out of place walking through the woods.

My mom wore baby's breath in her hair when she married my dad. I remember looking at their wedding photos as a little girl and thinking how absolutely stunning my mom looked. I always knew I wanted to incorporate baby's breath into my hair somehow. The flower crown Aleah created for me captured the essence of that little girl inside me who wanted wedding hair like her mom (with a modern, ethereal twist!).

Max and I wanted to feel comfortable, relaxed, and at peace (which was part of the reason we opted for a smaller home wedding versus a traditional wedding venue). My uncle, who also happens to be my godfather and one of my closest friends, married us. He really understands me and was so thrilled for us—it genuinely showed throughout the ceremony.

Bohemian Estate Wedding *171*

Allie & Collins

At the Winery

Allie and Collins had a vision of an extraordinary
destination wedding at a private winery, filled with
delicate touches, incredible music, and an unforgettable
dance party. Allie dreamed of a color story that was
soft and airy, while still being impactful and bold. We
tied in breezy muslin fabrics, with soft blue on the
invitation font, table runners, and our custom illustrated
pillows, and pale pinks in the flowers and stationery.

One of our favorite elements of Allie and Collins' invitation was the vellum overlay that gave a peek to the illustration underneath—which was a keepsake for guests to frame. The cohesion of the invitation continued and elements like their crest and winery illustration were pulled onto the cocktail napkins and printed pillows (which Allie and Collins now display in their home). Tables felt crisp and airy as well—with billowy blue satin and light white linens. Greenery overhead enhanced the chandeliers—adding a subtle garden touch.

Two bars greeted the guests; the craft cocktail bar included a mint julep topped with a scoop of crushed ice, in recognition of Collins' native Kentucky, and a luscious blackberry cocktail crafted for Allie to signify the end of summer. Regional beers on tap and wine produced from the vineyard were all served by lively bartenders, adding to the experience. Wine barrels and raw wood created the bar settings, and subtle touches of wheat in vases nodded to the surrounding wheat fields of Eastern Washington. The fabric-printed menus carried through to the bar, with two small muslin menus (by La Happy Design & Calligraphy) fluttering in the breeze.

After a scenic walk up to the ceremony setting at the top of the vineyard, which overlooked the rolling wheat fields and vines, Allie and Collins' guests were welcomed with flutes of bubbling champagne. The processional was played by a guitarist who later joined in with the incredible rocking band. The evening's festivities were so lively and fun—with guests insisting on taking to the dance floor before dinner was even served.

Allie's bouquet was created with white garden roses, white clover, and rose bush foliage.

Collins' boutonnière contained white tea roses, clover, and rose bush foliage.

What they ate and drank

Starters

Cauliflower ceviche

Roasted tomato, chili de árbol, shrimp

Albondiga on crostini

Dinner

Grilled peaches, balsamic, feta, and late summer greens

Pescado veracruz sobre arroz

Whole lamb with grilled naan, hummus, and late-summer grilled vegetables

Something Sweet

Assorted macarons and French delicacies

Custom "Oreo" cookies stamped with their wedding date

Libation Offerings

Champagne

Muddled blackberry lemonade

Mint juleps

Rosé

Wine offerings

Local beer on tap

Various gin, rum, vodka, whiskey, bourbon martinis

Collins explains how his expectations played out on his wedding day:

My number one priority was the actual ceremony. Knowing it was in such a beautiful surrounding and that it would be a surreal moment that would pass in a flash, I wanted to soak in the moment for as long as I could. The minimalism of the ceremony area and décor were in perfect contrast to the beautiful landscape of where we were getting married. Nature did the decorating atop the vineyard; nothing was overstated.

Our wedding reflected our story because of what was most important to us: friends, family, and our love. As a couple, we are very private with our feelings, so it meant a lot to us to be able to pour our hearts out to one another during our vows we wrote for one another. That moment was for us, and we didn't care who heard—in that moment it was just the two of us. Then the rest of the evening was for the ones we loved and who supported our love. The details for them, and their experience were very special for us.

It was important for us to make sure everyone was in the same place at the same time from the ceremony, to the champagne walk through the vineyard, to the cocktails after the wedding, and then finally the entrées and dancing. This flow was markedly important as we have been to countless weddings where you don't really know what to do next, or the bands starts playing while people are still waiting for food. The flow of our wedding was perfect, and after the ceremonial dances, the dance floor was charged with people until we had to shut it down.

––––––––––––––––

Guest entertainment was a top priority. Having a live band was something I insisted on as well as an open bar with signature cocktails but also the ability to pick the drink you want, and not be limited to beer or wine.

Nothing went wrong. And if it did, no one knew about it and it happened behind the scenes. Flow was so important to us for the overall wedding experience, as it kept people lively and entertained, and with the energy level up, and nothing going wrong, the night was spectacular. There could have been a kitchen fire going on and we or no one else ever knew, Valley & Co. kept anything like that at bay.

Mollie & Aaron

At Home on the Water

Dreaming up Mollie and Aaron's wedding weekend
was such a treat. Our goal was to combine Mollie's
Texas roots and Aaron's Northwest home, where they
were married. With guests traveling from across the
country to a small coastal town outside of Seattle,
comfort was a key in creating their experience.

The home where Aaron grew up is nestled between the woods and the water, which made for a picturesque setting for Mollie and Aaron's wedding. Guests were dropped off via shuttle at the top of the property and they meandered their way down through the gorgeous grounds and over a babbling brook to be greeted in a maze-like grove of trees with champagne and popcorn before the ceremony. Molly and Aaron said their vows overlooking the glassy waters, and guests enjoyed happy hour with croquet, a bean bag toss, and craft cocktails in the garden before continuing the maze to the dinner tent—a stately sailcloth tent perched on the water.

At nightfall, navy, mustard, chartreuse, and white shawls were given to the ladies on the dance floor, and all danced the night away to the Chris Friel Orchestra.

The night was warm with a slight breeze, and the lights of the tent flickered on the water after the sun went down. Such a memorable day and celebration capped with a totally magical evening.

What they ate and drank

Starters

Buttered popcorn and champagne

Spanish-fried chicken bites—buttermilk marinated and chili dusted, tossed with garlic-cumin butter and served with compressed celery

Lobster Pops—house-made brioche, béarnaise aioli, butter lettuce, garden flowers and crisp lobster cakes

Rhubarb tartlets—compressed rhubarb, pistachio shell, preserved lemon, whipped goat cheese and rhubarb gastrique

Oyster Bar—Northwest oysters on the half-shell with bergamot ice

Kumamoto Oyster with champagne gelee

"Hair of the Hog" Oyster shooters with bacon snow

Pacific Northwest cheese display with dried fruits, candied walnuts, artisan breads, and crackers

Dinner

Baby Arugula salad with strawberries, feta, crystallized wasabi, basil, and balsamic vinaigrette

Apple-smoked Vancouver Island salmon with summer stone fruit chutney

Chimichurri marinated slow-cooked petite tenderloin with chili-basil demi-glace and summer corn relish

Grilled summer corn, scallion butter, chili-lime aioli, cotija cheese, and cilantro pesto

Grilled summer garden veggies—basil pesto marinated and tossed with fresh herbs

House artisan breads with Sonoma sea salt butter

Something Sweet

Apple cake with caramel buttercream

Coconut cake with passion fruit buttercream

Libation Offerings

Moscow mule

Margaritas

Champagne

Beer

Wine

Mollie's bouquet was lush with Gatsby Moon green hydrangeas and hydrangea foliage, cream garden roses, and ferns.

Aaron's boutonnière contained green hydrangea and accenting fern leaves.

Mollie expressed her excitement for all of the scenes at their wedding:

We were really excited to have the wedding at Aaron's childhood home. It's such a special place that both of us have loved over the years, and to get married there was pure perfection. We wrote the entire ceremony, including our vows, and this was something that was really special for both of us. I also wanted to cut our wedding cake with the same silver knife that my parents cut their cake with at their wedding—it was engraved with their wedding date, May 29, 1971.

We really wanted elements of both our backgrounds in our wedding. We wanted to show off the PNW in all its glory in August, but also be true to my Texas roots. We loved the Texas and Washington painted corn-hole boards! So cute. Washington was represented by the oysters and flowers from the region, and we had sugar cookies in the shape of Texas that every guest could take with them or enjoy after dinner.

We had his and hers drinks that incorporate our dogs—a Moscow mule named the "Mushu Mule" and a spicy margarita named the "Konarita." I also really loved the detail at each of the table settings; the gold flatware, custom embroidered napkins, and beautiful plates and centerpieces really reflected our style. I also loved the handwritten place cards for our guests. They matched our invitations and had the greenery and floral touches!

———————

Getting ready together with my girlfriends was super fun. The "first look" was also really special—I'm so glad we chose to do that. Hanging out with each other just after the ceremony was one of my favorite parts as well. I was feeling overwhelmed with happiness, and also relieved that I didn't fall walking down the aisle!

Stephanie & Ronald

Classic Romance

When we began working with Stephanie and Ron, we were delighted at their vision of a timeless and romantic downtown Seattle wedding, one without trends and brimming with their own unique charm, as well as the charm of Seattle. Ronald hails from Kentucky and Stephanie is from the Seattle area, so many of the guests were traveling in from around the country (and world) to celebrate these two sweet physicians.

One of our jobs was to find a picturesque reception venue that really sang to the allure of old Seattle and that had all of the bells and whistles of an outstanding guest experience. The two historic venues chosen speak for themselves. The private Holy Names Academy was the site for the wedding ceremony and it boasts the most beautiful pale pink interior and incredible woodwork and stained glass. The Rainier Club, selected for the reception venue, has room after room of mystery, architecture, famous artwork, and a breathtaking ballroom.

Stephanie attended Holy Names Academy, and it was fitting that the ambiance of the chapel was aligned with her vision for the ceremony and reception décor—understated and classic, with soft and delicate touches and colors. We only enhanced the church setting with garden-inspired flowers like Koko Loko garden roses, hydrangeas, gladiolas, and scabiosas—all enchanting and colorful flowers that were rather muted for the space but complimented it so well.

The Rainier Club's iconic ballroom just begged for accent—which we accomplished by dressing it in white Chiavari chairs, satin linens, and everlasting centerpieces that made it possible for guests to enjoy the ambiance but which did not overwhelm the space. Their breathtaking wedding truly looks as if it could have taken place in the 1950s, current day, or even twenty years from now.

After guests departed the church ceremony, they made their way across town to the club, where three dapper butlers in classic white tuxedo jackets were awaiting their arrival with coupes filled with

left: Stephanie's bouquet was a beautiful creation of white scabiosa, white garden roses, pink tea roses, white gladiolas, and greenery.

above: Ronald's boutonnière was a delicate pink tea rose surrounded by greenery.

champagne. The old wood and brass fixtures of the club, the iconic elevators, and eclectic wallpaper, and the unbelievable chandeliers throughout the property lent to the timeless, yet stunning ambiance.

We knew it was important to Ronald and Stephanie to include their guests in the magic of the day, so in lieu of one large wedding cake, we suggested they cut into a smaller three-tiered cake for the ceremonial cake cutting. Guests were treated to ten-inch cakes set on each dining table on white ceramic pedestals. The cakes not only added a darling bit of décor, but they then became a conversation piece as guests shared and passed around the cakes and talked about the different flavors. It was an unexpected activity!

What they ate and drank

Starters

Fennel-apple salad with celery, toasted walnuts, arugula, pecorino and cider-mustard vinaigrette

Dinner

Tangerine-glazed salmon with a creamy pine nut sauce, whipped potatoes, and summer vegetables, or

Pepper and spice-rubbed beef tenderloin with a wild blackberry-syrah sauce, whipped potatoes and summer vegetables, or

Savory Tuscan vegetarian risotto with roasted tomatoes, baby squashes, grilled zucchini ribbons, and Parmesan cheese

Something Sweet

Carrot cake with cream cheese

Classic red velvet cake with cream cheese

Vanilla cake with summer raspberry filling

Lemon cake with summer raspberry filling

Libation Offerings

Canyon Road Winery, California: Chardonnay, Pinot Grigio, Merlot, Cabernet Sauvignon

Spirits: Belvedere vodka, Bombay Sapphire gin, Tanqueray gin, Maker's Mark bourbon, Johnny Walker Red Blended scotch, Captain Morgan's spiced rum, Sauza Blue agave tequila

Beer: Bud Light, Pyramid, Red Hook, Stella Artois, Beck's non-alcoholic

THE NUPTIAL MASS CELEBRATING THE UNION OF

STEPHANIE ANN ORTMAN

and

RONALD GLEN RACHO

IN THE SACRAMENT OF HOLY MATRIMONY

SATURDAY, THE TWENTY-SECOND OF JULY
TWO THOUSAND SEVENTEEN

HOLY NAMES ACADEMY CHAPEL
SEATTLE, WASHINGTON

WE HOPE THIS PROGRAM WILL SERVE AS A GUIDE TO TODAY'S
CEREMONY. FR. MULHOLLAND WILL ALSO PROVIDE GUIDANCE
TO ENCOURAGE YOUR PARTICIPATION IN THE LITURGY.

HOLY COMMUNION IS RECEIVED BY PRACTICING CATHOLICS.
EVEN IF YOU ARE NOT CATHOLIC, YOU ARE WELCOME TO COME
FORWARD DURING COMMUNION FOR A BLESSING IF DESIRED.
PLEASE CROSS YOUR ARMS OVER YOUR CHEST IF YOU WOULD
LIKE A BLESSING.

IN ORDER TO RESPECT THE DIGNITY OF THE CEREMONY, WE ASK
THAT THERE IS NO FLASH PHOTOGRAPHY DURING THE SERVICE.
ADDITIONALLY, PLEASE SILENCE ALL CELL PHONES AND OTHER
ELECTRONIC DEVICES.

MR. & MRS. STEPHEN ORTMAN
AND MR. & MRS. CHARITO RACHO
cordially invite you to attend the marriage of

STEPHANIE & RONALD

holy names academy chapel
728 21ST AVENUE EAST
SEATTLE, WASHINGTON 98112

reception to follow

Stephanie and Ronald commented on the various elements of their wedding:

The most important thing to us on our wedding day was being able to share the celebration of our marriage with our family and friends. The most memorable moment was committing to our vows in front everyone we love. The ceremony in the classic and timeless Holy Names Chapel was complemented by the beauty and vintage Seattle style of the reception venue at the Rainier Club.

There was so much excitement prior to the ceremony. We were so happy to see our friends and family enjoying their time in Seattle. For many of them, it was their first trip to Seattle. We really wanted to make the experience memorable for our family and guests.

———————

Many of the guests commented on how wonderful it was to have individual table-side cakes. They enjoyed tasting the different flavors and mingling with the other tables. What a surprise for them!

Tiffany & Chris

Modern Ballroom

Tiffany and Chris's wedding was a fun-filled fête, with experiences around every corner and throughout each scene. As we worked together for two years, our goal was to create a gorgeous wedding that was stylish and splendid, while maintaining a level of comfort and understated elegance. Welcoming guests from across the world to Seattle meant finding a quintessential Seattle venue that could offer comfort and an ideally central location. The Four Seasons was the perfect property for guest comfort, style, and for the sweeping views of the waterfront below, including the now iconic Great Wheel.

Tiffany and Chris had in mind a very distinctive look and feeling they wanted for their wedding, but they laid their trust in us to create an incredible experience and to run with their ideas and surprise them with many of the details. It was a day of sensory experiences: from the spectacular champagne tower to the lively band, the multi-course Northwest-inspired meal, to the cigar roller and the surprise of the Great Wheel below the Four Seasons lighting up at dark with their wedding colors—navy and gold!

La Happy Designs & Calligraphy created a stately acrylic escort board that chicly displayed guests' tables, where they were met with lucite table numbers filled with illustrated sea creatures and calligraphy. That motif was subtly carried throughout on the welcome totes, the long menus on each place setting, the drink stirrers, and the printed cocktail napkins and matches on the bar.

Tiffany's gown came with its own story. It was worn by her mother in the 1980s and by her grandmother in the 1950s. The lace, kept dry for decades, was surprisingly well preserved. This gown was one of the first conversations we had with Tiffany—she was certain that she wanted to carry on her family tradition and wear this same wedding gown, but with a few slight modernized details.

Guests wined and dined, and were treated to a live music dance party by the Chris Friel Orchestra, a lively group of extremely talented musicians who know how to bring the party. There's really nothing better than sitting back and watching the orchestra rocking—and guests in their best formal attire shimmying and boogying into the night.

Their farewell was a gold confetti-filled au revoir, with guests all gathering and cheering for Tiffany and Chris while popping confetti cannons!

The party didn't end then, either. Guests headed downstairs into the tavern for a late night after-party with more food and drink before calling it a night. Not only was Tiffany and Chris's wedding day brimming with sentiment and formality, but it was highlighted by comfort and unforgettable experiences for their guests.

Tiffany envisioned a clean and timeless bouquet that was constructed with panda anemones and tied in a navy satin ribbon with a sweet bow.

Chris's boutonnière was made from baby's breath and secured with a pearl tie pin belonging to Tiffany's grandfather.

What they ate and drank

Starters

Dungeness crab cake with piquillo pepper aioli and heirloom tomato

Salad with Belgian endive, butter lettuce, pine nut brittle, and white balsamic vinaigrette

Dinner

Spiced rubbed beef tenderloin with baby carrots, haricots verts, gratin potatoes in a red wine demi reduction or

Saffron-poached halibut, fennel, asparagus, gratin potatoes in lemon crème or

Grilled vegetable ravioli, roasted eggplant, oven-dried tomatoes in a roasted tomato sauce

Something Sweet

Carrot cake with vanilla bean diplomat filling and cream cheese icing or

Almond genoise cake with raspberry filling and buttercream icing

Libation Offerings

Poema Brut Cava, Spain (Champagne Tower)

Tiffany Rosé All Day - Sauza Silver Tequila, St. Germaine, Grapefruit Juice, topped with Bubbles

Rain Killer - Pusser's Rum, Pineapple Juice, Orange Juice, Cream of Coconut, Fresh Grated Nutmeg

Nick and Neah Valley
1428 Magnolia Drive
Seattle, Washington
98104

Tiffany
Malay

i can't think of anything but nights with you.
I want them to be warm so long
when we can be together all of our lives —
Zelda Fitzgerald

FIND YOUR SEAT

Mr. and Mrs. Douglas Wade Chaney
request the honour of your presence
at the Nuptial Mass uniting their daughter

Tiffany Rose
and
Mr. Christopher Michael Malay

Saturday, the third of June
two thousand seventeen
at two o'clock in the afternoon

Immaculate Conception Church
820 18th Avenue
Seattle, Washington

Love,
Chris & Tiffany
June 3, 2017

The Future Mr. a
1515 15th St. N
Washington, D

Save

TIFFANY CHANEY

to b
06

SEATTLE, WASHINGTON

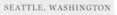

Kaylee
Smith

Kim
Smith

Tiffany was thrilled with how her wedding plans were played out:

I have always loved *The Great Gatsby* and F. Scott Fitzgerald's writings. Fast forward to after we got engaged, and started imagining our actual wedding. We agreed on some key things: we would get married in a beautiful cathedral-style church, the reception would be in Seattle, it would be in June, we wanted to have a venue with a view, and we definitely needed a wedding planner!

We then jumped on to some of the harder parts; mainly, the look and feel of our wedding. Since a good portion of our wedding guests would be coming from out of town and we both love Seattle, Chris had the wonderful idea of incorporating Seattle elements into each part of the wedding.

We had to include Frank (our French bulldog) in the wedding plans because he is named after my grandpa. Frank has been a huge part of our relationship; he has a lot of health issues and has had five major surgeries over the time that Chris and I have been together. I knew Chris was the one when I saw how well he could take care of my fur child, who is now our fur child!

I had lost my grandma recently, and my grandpa lost his battle with Parkinson's the December after we got engaged. Together in their prime, they were the most glamorous couple I had the privilege of knowing, and I would often flip through their albums from the 1950s as if they were a catalog. My grandma was always dressed in such a classic yet glamorous way that you couldn't help but be drawn to her. My grandpa was equally. Shortly after getting married, they could be seen zooming around Tacoma in their Jag. Their carefree life and impeccable taste were something that I wanted reflected throughout my wedding.

Combining these items together, we landed on a wedding design that we could only describe as Gatsby visits the Northwest in the 1950s. We wanted something that had the allure and fun of Gatsby's parties, the classic glamor of my grandparents in the '50s, and all the beauty of the Northwest.

planning roundup

Detail Planning

Regardless of your wedding budget or style, details can
be carried throughout that hold significant meaning
to your wedding plans. Here is a benchmark for some
of the basic key details and moments to keep in mind
when starting down the road of planning and designing
the elements and special tones of your story. We've
left room for you to write down some of your ideas.

getting ready:

Stage your attire in a way that feels exceptionally special—work with your planner, a stylist, or friend or family member to gather your trousseau and thoughtfully display your veil and gown, style your perfume and jewelry with flowers. Stage a suit or tux with cologne and accessories like cuff links and a watch the night before the wedding. Plan time for your photographer to capture these details before the festivities and portraits begin. Plan sufficient time before your portraits and ceremony to enjoy the surroundings, to be with your family or wedding party, and to soak up the beauty around you.

basic comforts for the guests:

Where are they staying?

Where do guests put their gifts or cards?

What are they to wear?

Where are the restrooms?

How are they getting to the wedding?

How will your guests travel between venues?

Where do guests put their coats
at the wedding?

How do guests know their seating
assignments at any of the venues?

the guests' entrance:

What will your guests be greeted with (if anything)? Sparkling water? A fanciful cocktail? Hors d'oeuvres?

_____

_____

_____

What welcome gifts or favors will be provided?

_____

_____

_____

What sounds will they hear (funky favorites, romantic piano, organ music)?

_____

_____

_____

Review your plans to make sure that you have answered these initial questions through your wedding website, your invitation suite, and with best laid plans on the wedding day with signage, greeters who can help to guide guests, assigned seating, and clear stations. People generally arrive and are thirsty after travel—to echo our greeting, staging a simple table with water carafes and cups is an easy way to address a comfort that puts people at ease when they first walk in the door and sets the tone for hospitality.

_____

_____

_____

_____

_____

_____

_____

_____

_____

the ceremony:

Consider details like signage that illustrates how the ceremony is laid out, or have special people pass out programs to your guests. Do you want thoughtful readings by people close to you, or even an unexpected musical twist (a la the *Love Actually* wedding scene)? The ceremony is your time to reflect and share, as much or as little as you choose.

_____

_____

_____

_____

_____

_____

_____

_____

the cocktail hour:

If it's your style, bring in fun games like croquet or a chess table. Fill this time with saying thanks to your guests or create unexpected activities like a caricature artist or a steel drummer. No matter how formal or informal your event, guests will find happiness in surprise.

_____

_____

the bar:

Serve your favorite signature cocktails but also delight guests with beer flights or whiskey tastings, or bubbly paired with appetizers. Personalize things like cocktail menus and napkins with your favorite quote or monogram.

_____

_____

Stock restrooms with fresh flowers and baskets of mints, mouth wash, Band-Aids, sunscreen, and lotion.

_____

_____

the reception:

The look and feeling of your dining experience can be built on comfort and be dressed with simplicity, opulence, or timeless details. These details will shine through with your escort display (which tells guests which table they'll be seated at), the dining chairs, your table configurations (all rounds, a mix of café-style seating, long family-style tables, or squares), linen color and texture, and the flowers or décor you stage on each table. Details can continue through lighting and music, and what is present on place settings (take-home favors, hand-written thank you notes, or a simple napkin).

the farewell:

This is a moment that shouldn't be overlooked. Have someone assigned to gather the guests to bid you au revoir with fireworks, confetti, or the fanfare of cheers!

Our Style Exercise

Rank by priority what experiences are most key to your wedding story:

_____ The ceremony and your vows

_____ The venue or destination location

_____ Activities and experiences that conform to family traditions

_____ Sensory experiences that highlight your likes and hobbies (music, objects, videos)

_____ The dining experience

_____ The look and ambiance—including flowers, linens, textures, and lighting

_____ The entertainment—including ceremony musicians and music throughout

_____ The party aspect

_____ Unexpected treats for your guests (like activities we have mentioned)

_____ Guest comfort

_____ The attire of you and your wedding party

_____ The photography or videography of your wedding

_____ A unique and spectacular invitation suite

"I think every bride will look back at her wedding at some point and giggle about the elements that demonstrated the trends of the time she was married but I also believe that brides should put thought into their own personal style and let that shine throughout the wedding. If she takes the time to define her style to the vendors in her wedding, it will really shine through."

—Kimberly Schlegel Whitman

What season or month of the year have you always thought you would like your wedding?

_____

How have you always envisioned your ceremony (family church, formal mass, in a park)?

_____

Who do you want to marry you (priest, judge, family member)?

_____

Who do you want to walk with you in the processional?

_____

Do you want traditional or hand-written vows?

_____

How long do you want your wedding ceremony to be?

_____

What tone do you want for your ceremony?

_____

What do you enjoy most at weddings?

_____

What is something you absolutely don't want at your wedding?

_____

What does your perfect night out with friends look like?

_____

How can you incorporate that perfect night into your wedding day?

_____

What are ten of your all-time favorite foods?

_____

_____

What are five words you would want to use to describe your whole wedding experience?

_____

What are five words you would want to use to describe the visual aspects of your wedding?

_____

What kind of décor do you have in your home or want to have in your home that you would want to see at your wedding?

_____

_____

Find 10-15 photos that really resonate with you—and try to avoid photos from other weddings online (or stick to just one or two that really speak to the overall look that you've been dreaming of). These images can be from travel adventures, memorable dining experiences, an incredible dessert that still makes your mouth water, moments of your life that have stuck with you, a picturesque garden that left you in awe, the building you live in, and anything else that evokes emotion. Does your collection of images say regal and refined? More casual and edited? Stylish and off of the runway? Or everything in between?

_____

"On the actual wedding day, literally everything lends itself to communicating personal style. My advice would be to pick the things that are most important to you and focus on them. Maybe it's the flowers and the tablescapes. Maybe it's the booze and the band. Maybe it's the dress and accessories. Whatever it is, make those essentials the most personal and special they can be."

—Alexandra Macon

Parting Letter for Soon-to-be-Newlyweds

We are thankful that you have read *Storied Weddings* and are hopeful that you have found great inspiration, bookmarked ideas, jotted down planning tips, and feel inspired beyond measure. We hope you find yourself flicking through the pages time and time again. For our industry peers, we hope that we have inspired you as well and that you share in many of our sentiments. When we began on our journey of wedding planning right out of college, little did we know that it would take us on this awesome adventure, having the distinct honor of being part of countless couples' most intimate moments, being welcomed and treated like family, and having such an honor of being entrusted to plan and create such incredibly special and personalized weddings. We have experienced and learned so much. Even now we often sit back and relish in the fact that this is what we do for a living. That's pretty special.

In a sea of incredible ideas, please remember that your wedding is to be a celebration of you, your tastes, your likes, and a celebration of you by your families and friends, and should be planned with that thought in mind. Make every effort to create experiences for you and for your guests that are representations of you—that sing oh, this is so us! While wedding "rules" have existed for centuries, you needn't conform to them if that's not your cup of tea. You may throw tradition out the window or choose to carry historic wedding traditions throughout each moment of your day.

However you decide to plan the scenes of your wedding, you can most definitely find cohesion in variety—if you try. Guests will delight in wearing tuxes and noshing on cheeseburgers as much as they would enjoy a five-course plated meal with all of the bells and whistles, if they know that the day is perfectly you.

So, when you plan, think about your favorite songs, flowers that bring you joy, family memories, quirky ideas, and sentimental touches. Whether your wedding is a weekend-long casual soirée, a formal fête, a brunch gathering, or the party of the century, the beauty is that it is all yours. Your hallmark, your storied wedding.

Cheers,
Aleah and Nick

I Remember When . . .

Fond Memories from Our Contributors

I remember when . . . my husband shocked everyone, including me, at our rehearsal dinner. When it was his turn to give a toast, he moved his place setting to the side and hopped up on to the table. The table was long and large and he walked all the way around it, navigating his way through floral arrangements, to say something special to every single person at the table. I'll never forget it!

—Kimberly Schlegel Whitman

I remember when I saw my husband for the first time on our wedding day. We decided to see each other before the ceremony, which I am so happy we did. It allowed us to get the emotions and nerves out and additionally take some pretty special photographs before the rush of the guests and the party took over. I highly recommend that private time.

—Ceci Johnson

I remember when . . . all of the guests at our wedding were dancing on that warm July evening to "Shout" played by our incredible band. I remember seeing Nick for the first time at our first look moment and just laughing together—perhaps a little nervously, but so happily. I remember thinking how lucky I was to be marrying my best friend. I remember my mom and dad so proudly walking me down the aisle. I remember dancing in a hilariously "semi-choreographed" dance with my younger brother at our wedding to Norah Jones and my older brother cutting in. I remember the gorgeous colors of blue of the ocean and the sky on that day. The sounds of laughter, the wafting smell of delicious food, and our favorite people surrounding us in celebration.

—Aleah Valley

One of my couples was quite literally obsessed with Chick-fil-A. Their wedding was in Virginia and, being New Englanders, the only time they could indulge in their favorite treat was during wedding planning meetings. As a surprise to the groom, the bride wanted to have the Chick-fil-A cow hand out late-night snacks. That alone was priceless, but when I went to help get the person into her costume, it turns out she had been given a brand new mask—with no eye holes! I had to hold the cow's hand the entire time to lead her onto the packed dance floor and make sure she didn't fall over or bump into anything. It was an amazing surprise for everyone especially the groom, but the story was made even better when I told them about the mask the next day!

—Jacin Fitzgerald

From our client weddings, we fondly remember Ben and Marquinta's hands-down best entrance into a first dance, Tiffany and Chris's epic grand exit, Chris and Kelly's adorable grandmothers as flower girls, Jeny and Jeff's dear friend reading from Dr. Seuss during their ceremony, the whiskey incident at Emily and Ryen's woodsy wedding, countless dance floors that have literally come apart from dance parties that legends are made from, and the ceremonies and special moments we have had the honor of witnessing.

—Aleah and Nick

Some of my favorite wedding memories are when the pressure is on to complete the design and the entire Intrigue team comes together. I remember one particular wedding that required four additional centerpieces created just twenty minutes before guests were scheduled to arrive. My team certainly could have been stressed, but instead they were excited and eager to take on the challenge. For fifteen ferocious minutes, clippers were clipping and flowers were flying as the designers created beauty out of what had been set aside for catering displays. The pieces were placed on tables just moments before guests arrived.

—Sarah C. Campbell

At my best friend's wedding, the bride's niece decided that she needed to be the center of attention during the very formal, Catholic ceremony. She started doing twists and twirls at the altar, just as the bride and groom were exchanging vows. We (all the bridesmaids and groomsmen) couldn't stop looking at each other from across the aisle and giggling while we all held it together to watch the vows.

—Anna Price Olson

Contributors

SARAH C. CAMPBELL
Intrigue Design
www.intrigue-designs.com

JESS LEVIN CONROY, FOUNDER & CEO OF
     CARATS & CAKE
www.caratsandcake.com

JACIN FITZGERALD, FOUNDER OF JACIN FITZGERALD EVENTS
www.jacinfitzgerald.com

CECI JOHNSON, FOUNDER AND CREATIVE DIRECTOR OF
     CECI NEW YORK
CECI NEW YORK
www.cecinewyork.com

ALEXANDRA MACON, CO-FOUNDER OF OVER THE MOON AND WEDDINGS
     EDITOR AT VOGUE.COM

ANNA PRICE OLSON, REAL WEDDINGS EDITOR, *BRIDES*
www.brides.com

KIMBERLY SCHLEGEL WHITMAN,
     AUTHOR AND LIFESTYLE EXPERT
www.kimberlywhitman.com

CAMILLE WYNN, FOUNDER OF THE DRESS THEORY
www.thedresstheory.com

Acknowledgments

We are beyond humbled that we have this magical opportunity to publish *Storied Weddings*. It has been a dream for as long as we can remember to put our work out into the world and share our knowledge, creativity, and approach to telling wedding stories in a printed book. This is an absolute honor and we still feel like we're dreaming!

The "& Company" in our name helps us to represent the many people who have embarked on this journey with us and continue to support us in our crazy endeavors, alongside the weddings and events that we plan and design, and our many other creative projects. To the photographers, musicians, venue directors, catering teams, dishwashers, valet parkers, stationery designers, and everyone who helps to bring the magic of a wedding day to life, thank you!

Happy Saunders, you are a gem! We appreciate your upbeat attitude, your endless hard work, and your beautiful creative skills. Thank you!

Katelynn Bacher Rowe, our thanks for your cheerful presence and hard work in Napa.

We are grateful to the late Gibbs Smith, founder of Gibbs Smith Publishing, for seeing creativity in so many incredible authors. We are honored to rub elbows with and to be represented by such a stellar publishing house and to be in such good company.

Many thanks to Katie Killebrew, our outstanding editor, who was just as excited about publishing our book as we have been! We thank you for seeing something unique and fresh and for believing in us. Thank you for your guidance and the tools and your expertise to create such a gorgeous book.

To Scott and Ashlee O'Malley, thank you for your friendship and for partnering with us on the fabulous weddings within these pages and for capturing the details and the stories of some of our favorite couples so effortlessly. We know how hard you both work behind the scenes and that results in timeless images and the story of each couple told so perfectly. Thank you for your partnership and collaboration on this book. You are such a talent to this industry. What a fun adventure it has been!

Marcy Blum, thank you for penning the foreword to our book. We have long admired your attitude and honesty, your talents, and the remarkable road you have paved for our industry. Your humor, creativity, and dedication to spectacular weddings and parties continually raises the bar in our industry as a whole. You are so warm and wonderful to be around—thank you!

Thank you to the artists who contributed so much to creating the beautiful art to be photographed. From the paper goods to the calligraphy, the wedding gowns, properties, drinks, and details in between, you all helped us to meet and exceed our vision for these weddings and our book. Thank you to our contributors Kimberly Schlegel Whitman, Ceci Johnson, Jess Levin Conroy, Camille Wynn, Jacin Fitzgerald, Anna Price Olson, Sarah C. Campbell, and Alexandra Macon. We admire you all and appreciate your friendship and expertise.

To all of our amazing couples and clients, we thank you for letting us play a role in planning your weddings. Entrusting us with your stories means so much. Thank you to our five sweet couples featured in these pages for sharing your stories in the book.

Mollie and Aaron, we still smile when we think back on the planning process with you. Your humor and kindness were felt through each moment of your wedding. You two make such a stellar couple. We feel like we know both of your pooches and are happy we got to incorporate them into the wedding!

To Ash and Max, you guys are way too much fun. Thank you for entrusting your day to us and for giving Nick the task of bringing a menagerie of farm animals into the wedding. We will always think back on this and laugh out loud! Thank you for sharing Patty with us—what a kick!

Tiffany and Chris, what a fun journey we had together! Two years in the making, your wedding was such a phenomenal party and we loved every moment. Your champagne tower was legendary. Your getaway epic. We adore you both.

Ronald and Stephanie, working together was such a pleasure and we value your thoughts and approach to planning. We appreciate your vision and the ideals of throwing a classic and special wedding. We are so happy to know you both.

To Allie and Collins, what to say? We had so much fun with you during the planning process and on our visit to wine country together. Thank you for your humor, your trust, and your gratitude.

To our parents, all of our gratitude and thanks to you for never letting us falter on our dreams and goals, as crazy as they may seem sometimes. We absolutely could not do what we do without you. Thank you for believing in us, for your unwavering support and encouragement, and for being such incredible parents and grandparents.

Mom and Dad, thank you for instilling in me the importance of balancing dedication, hard work, and fun in life. I am forever grateful for you. —A.

Mom, thank you so much for all your support and grace. I appreciate beyond words everything you have done for me. —N.

Thank you to our families and friends for the encouragement and support throughout our adventures.

To Ava and Bennett, we love you both to the moon and back! You are our greatest accomplishments. You are such sweet, caring, creative, and smart kiddos and it is so important for us to instill in you the values of family, tradition, hard work, creativity, and humility. We are excited that you both have had a part in this book, though you might be a bit too little to remember! We love you.

Cheers,
Aleah and Nick

Resources

DESIGNS

Blue skirt and lace top
Sweet Caroline Styles
sweetcarolinestyles.com

GARDEN CHARM

Planning, design, and floral
Valley & Company Events
valleyandco.com

Property
Carnation Farms
carnationfarms.org

Dresses used
Dress Theory
thedresstheory.com

Rings
Victor Barbone
victorbarbone.com

Linens
La Tavola
latavolalinen.com

Cakes
Lilac Cake Boutique
lilaccakeboutique.com

Garden gown
Hailey Paige
From Dress Theory

Monogrammed napkins
Halo Home by Kimberly Schlegel
  Whitman
halohomebyksw.com

Greenery
Continental Floral Greens
cfgreens.com

Garden stationery
Momental Designs
momentaldesigns.com

Garden roses
Grace Rose Farm
gracerosefarm.com

Gold leafy hair garland
Twiggs & Honey
twiggsandhoney.com

Cheese platter
Lisa Dupar Catering
duparandcompany.com

Candies
The Confectionery
theconfectionery.com

SOMETHING BLUE

Property
Private Estate

Planning, design, and floral
Valley & Company Events
valleyandco.com

Tent/glasses
CORT Party Rental
cortpartyrental.com

White chairs and candles
Crate & Barrel
crateandbarrel.com

Cake
Lilac Cake Boutique
lilaccakeboutique.com

Monogrammed napkins
Halo Home by Kimberly Schlegel
  Whitman
halohomebyksw.com

Greenery
Continental Floral Greens
cfgreens.com

Dress
The Dress Theory
thedresstheory.com

Catering
Lisa Dupar Catering
lisaduparcatering.com

Stationery
Momental Designs
momentaldesigns.com

Ring Box
The Mrs. Box
themrsbox.com

OLD WORLD ROMANCE

Planning, design, and floral
Valley & Company Events
valleyandco.com

Venue
Whetstone Wine Cellars
whetstonewinecellars.com

Dress
Sweet Caroline Styles
sweetcarolinestyles.com

Tabletop rentals
Theoni Collection
theonicollection.com

Linens
La Tavola
latavolalinen.com

Model
Audrey Bomar
Scout Model Agency
Scouttm.com

Hair and Makeup
Elegante Beaute - Hair and Makeup by
  Linda
elegantebeaute.com

Stationery
Momental Designs
momentaldesigns.com

Car
Calispeed Motorsports
calispeedcars.com

NAPA WINERY

Planning, design, and floral
Valley & Company Events
valleyandco.com

Venue and food
Ramekins
ramekins.com

Stationery
Momental Designs
momentaldesigns.com

Tabletop rentals
Theoni Collection
theonicollection.com

Linens
La Tavola
latavolalinen.com

Dress
Sweet Caroline Styles
sweetcarolinestyles.com

Copper Bells
Ravenna Gardens
ravennagardens.com

Model
Audrey Bomar
Scout Model Agency
Scouttm.com

Hair and makeup
Elegante Beaute - Hair and Makeup by
  Linda
elegantebeaute.com

Car
Calispeed Motorsports
calispeedcars.com

Estate

Planning, design, and floral
Valley & Company Events
valleyandco.com

Venue
Admiral's House
theadmiralshouse.com

Rentals
CORT Party Rental
cortpartyrental.com

Stationery and calligraphy
Libby Tipton
libbytipton.com

Dress
The Dress Theory
thedresstheory.com

Shoes
Bella Belle Shoes
bellabelleshoes.com

Linens
La Tavola
latavolalinen.com

Cake
Midori Bakery
midoribakery.com

Modern

Planning, design, and floral
Valley & Company Events
valleyandco.com

Rentals
CORT Party Rental
cortpartyrental.com

Linens
La Tavola
latavolalinen.com

Stationery
La Happy Design & Calligraphy
lahappy.com

Cake
Midori Bakery
midoribakery.com

Cocktail
Perfect Pour Cocktail Co.
perfectpourseattle.com

Collections

1 Invitations and Monograms

Whale crest
Libby Tipton
libbytipton.com

Winery invitation
Izzy Girl Design
izzygirl.com

Blue/white calligraphy
Laura Hooper Calligraphy
lhcalligraphy.com

Botanical suite
CECI NEW YORK
cecinewyork.com

Black-and-white invitation suite
La Happy Design & Calligraphy
lahappy.com

Monogrammed napkin
La Happy Design & Calligraphy
Ballard Embroidery
ballardembroidery.com

Monogrammed hankies
Oatmeal Lace
oatmeallace.com

Painted old world invitation
Momental Designs
momentaldesigns.com

2 Venue Styles

Whetstone Wine Cellars
whetstonewinecellars.com

Ramekins
ramekins.com

Roche Harbor Resort
rocheharbor.com

River Terrace Inn
riverterraceinn.com

The Chateau at DeLille Cellars, the Lill Family Estate
delillecellars.com

3 Ceremony, Flower Girls & Ring Bearers

Calligraphy/wreath
Laura Hooper Calligraphy
lhcalligraphy.com

Programs
Libby Tipton
libbytipton.com

4 Style & Heirlooms

Rings
Victor Barbone
victorbarbone.com

Mustard gown/top
Sweet Caroline Styles
sweetcarolinestyles.com

Hair and makeup
Elegante Beaute - Hair and Makeup by Linda
elegantebeaute.com

Dress form
Found Vintage Rentals
foundrentals.com

Shoes
Bella Belle Shoes
bellabelleshoes.com

Boutonniere calligraphy
La Happy Design & Calligraphy
lahappy.com

5 Personalize It (Favors)

Olive leaf crest in welcome box
Izzy Girl Design
izzygirl.com

Citrus/butterflies/hanging tags/garden tags
Libby Tipton
libbytipton.com

Chukar Cherries
chukar.com

DRY Soda
drysparkling.com

Maury Island Farms jams
mauryislandfarm.com

Cookies
Ruth-Anne Ford Cakes & Confections
ruthanneford.com

Boxed chocolates
Fran's Chocolates
franschocolates.com

6 Cocktail Hour & After Party

Rentals of furniture/bar
Found Vintage Rentals
foundrentals.com

Greenery
Continental Floral Greens
cfgreens.com

Tabletop rentals
Theoni Collection
theonicollection.com

Appetizers
River Terrace Inn - restaurant
riverterraceinn.com

Fried chicken and oysters
Lisa Dupar Catering
lisaduparcatering.com

Cocktails
Perfect Pour Cocktail Co.
perfectpourseattle.com

7 Wedding Desserts

Whimsical cake/white marbled/
painted floral cake
Lila Cake Boutique
lilacakeboutique.com

Towering Cake/White Berry
Ruth-Anne Ford Cakes and Confections
ruthanneford.com

Dessert Display
Tallant House Fine Sweets & Other
    Treats
tallanthouse.com

Doughnuts
Cupcake Royale
cupcakeroyale.com

Macarons
Trophy Cupcakes & Party
trophycupcakes.com

Popsicles
Seattle Pops
seattlepops.com

Pies/tiny cakes
Sweetie Pies Napa
sweetiepies.com

Sliced cake
Midori Bakery
midoribakery.com

8 Receptions/Place Settings

Rentals
CORT Party Rental
cortpartyrental.com

Rose print
La Happy Design & Calligraphy
lahappy.com

Favor
Fran's Chocolates
franschocolates.com

Venue 1

Greenery
Continental Floral Greens
cfgreens.com

Linens
Choice Linens
choicelinens.com

Venue 2

The Chateau at DeLille Cellars, a
Lill Family Estate
delillecellars.com

Rentals
CORT Party Rental
cortpartyrental.com

Linens
Choice Linens
choicelinens.com

Venue 3

Roche Harbor Resort
rocheharbor.com

9 Music Style

Victrola
Found Vintage Rentals
foundrentals.com

Guitarist
Patricio Contreras
pguitarra@aol.com
theherbfarm.com/about/music

Blue Wave Band
bluewaveband.com

Band
Chris Friel Orchestra
chrisfriel.com

Real Wedding vendor credits

Bohemian Estate Wedding

Planning, design, and floral
Valley & Company Events
valleyandco.com

Venue
bride's family home

Stationery and calligraphy
La Happy Design & Calligraphy
lahappy.com

Bride's dress
Dress Theory
thedresstheory.com

Groom's suit
Nordstrom

Hair and makeup
Erin Skipley Hair and Makeup
erinskipley.com

Tent and rentals/linens
CORT Party Rental
www.cortpartyrental.com

Furniture
Vintage Ambiance
vintageambiance.com

Candles
Glassybaby
glassybaby.com

Favors
Fran's Chocolates
franschocolates.com

Wedding cake
The Sweet Side,
thesweetsideseattle.com

Catering
Lisa Dupar Catering
duparandcompany.com

DJ
Michael Garcia
miguelrockwell.com

Video
Magical Touch Media
magicaltouchmedia.com

At the Winery

Planning, design, and floral
Valley & Company Events
valleyandco.com

Venue
private winery

Stationery/calligraphy
La Happy Design & Calligraphy
lahappy.com

Bride's dress
The White Dress

Flower girl dresses
Hello Alyss
helloalyss.com

Linens
Choice Linens
choicelinens.com

Furniture
Fleurissant
fleurissant.com

Favors
Antica Farmacista
anticafarmacista.com

Desserts
Walla Walla Bread Company
w2breadco.com